G000108271

Long Distance Walks
in the Pyrenees

LONG DISTANCE WALKS IN THE
PYRENEES

CHRIS TOWNSEND

SERIES EDITOR JOHN CLEARE

The Crowood Press

First published in 1991 by
The Crowood Press Ltd
Gipsy Lane, Swindon
Wiltshire SN2 6DQ

British Library Cataloguing in Publication Data
Townsend, Chris 1949–
    Long Distance Walks in the Pyrenees.
    1. Europe. Pyrenees – Visitors' guides
    I. Title
    914.6520483

    ISBN 1 85223 391 5

Photographs by Chris Townsend.
Black and white photographs taken from colour transparencies.

Series editor John Cleare

Typeset by Columns Design & Production Services Ltd., Reading
Printed and bound in Great Britain by BPCC Hazell Books, Aylesbury

Acknowledgements

Most of my walks in the Pyrenees have been made in the company of others and I would like to thank Graham Huntington, Alain Kahan and Mark Edgington for their friendship and also, perhaps especially, for putting up with my photographic requirements. It cannot be easy to stop or even to go back a few steps during a steep climb because someone wants to take a picture!

This book is enhanced by the fine maps, the work of Don Sargeant. My thanks go out to him.

During my trips to the Pyrenees I have met many local people and other walkers; all have added to my appreciation of the area and I am most grateful for their friendliness.

On all my walks I have relied on trail guides as well as on maps for information, ideas and route details. Much of their work has been incorporated into this book via my walks, so my thanks to Kev Reynolds, Georges Veron and Arthur Battagel and the various anonymous authors of the GR10 topo guide.

Contents

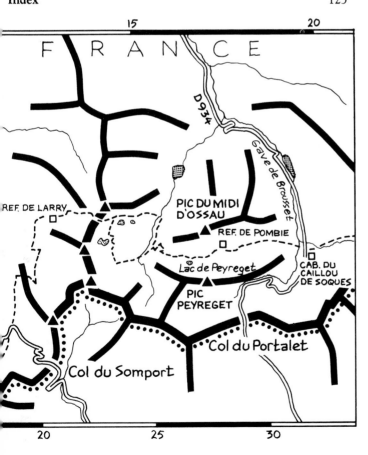

Preface

'Travel', wrote Francis Bacon nearly four hundred years ago, 'is a part of education.' But it is also far more than that. Many see the burgeoning travels of today's common man as an important key to international understanding and world harmony. Others – more pessimistic, yet perhaps more perceptive – see the profligate scatter of the tourist dollar as enriching local economies while despoiling subtle cultures and eroding fragile environments, a typical Third World scenario yet one recognizable even here in Europe. There is truth in both views. Travel is surely a two-edged sword.

Thus we who travel and enjoy the wild places – at risk by their very definition – bear a heavy responsibility. It is up to us to do the right thing, to set the right example, and to thoughtfully champion the cause of the wilderness. It is all too easy to kill the goose that lays the golden eggs. A case in point was the closure of the exquisite Nanda Devi Sanctuary by the Indian Government in 1983 after its very essence had been jeopardized by excessive use and environmental pollution. In Europe too there are comparable problems but commercial greed and people pressures have ensured that frequently it is already too late.

Leave nothing but footprints, take nothing but photographs is a dictum originally coined in North America and no less applicable elsewhere. Luckily much of the beautiful range described in this book is still relatively unspoilt – by European standards. National Parks, both French and Spanish, protect large areas of the Pyrenees and their sensible regulations help to minimize the pressure that inevitably afflicts all European beauty spots. Such rules as no wild camping within an hour's walk from a road seem to me to be eminently wise and should be observed scrupulously. The future of the wild places is in our hands.

This book is one of our on-going series of Long Distance Walks titles which sets out to encourage the discerning traveller to undertake and enjoy journeys on foot through many of the world's wild places. Typically the series covers mountains or upland country because that is where the most interesting routes are usually found, and with difficulties and commitments to suit most tastes. It does so always mindful of environmental considerations.

Most travel books fall into one of two categories. Some are guidebooks pure and simple, usually useful and at best even interesting if hardly a 'good read'. Others are narrative accounts, readable, fascinating, often extremely entertaining, but typically disdainfully ignoring any desire of readers to repeat the journey themselves. Hopefully our series embraces something of both, entertaining and enthusing – albeit itchy-footedly – while helping the traveller with first-hand practical advice and crucial information.

Chris Townsend, our author, is a professional travel journalist and editor who has returned to the Pyrenees time and again for over a decade in between a series of major journeys through other, supposedly more exotic, wilderness areas throughout the world. Obviously he considers this beautiful mountain range is very special – and as one who has only recently made its acquaintance I can certainly agree!

Sharing his travels and enthusiasm on ten superb itineraries you will visit many of the region's classic landmarks and features. You will experience much of the delight that our Victorian forebears found when they first explored Europe's great mountain ranges and which is now, alas, so elusive in the Alps. You will certainly enjoy!

John Cleare

Introduction

When the usual British summer hill weather, replete with mist, moisture and midges, forces my thoughts abroad and I long for dry, clear, sunny mountain days, high camps in delectable cirques by cool mountain lakes overlooking spectacular views and valley camps in shady woodland by tumbling, pure refreshing streams and heights glinting in the sunlight through the green canopy, then one place, one range of mountains comes to mind: the Pyrenees.

These are summer mountains *par excellence*; generally dry, usually hot and with a clarity of air rare in the damp, haze-ridden island skies of home, a unique mix of the Mediterranean and the Alpine, as is appropriate for a range that forms the frontier between Spain and France. The Pyrenees are not one uniform mountain chain, however; within the narrow strip that defines them there are many separate massifs with their own clear identity and an incredible diversity of landscapes. The light, airy limestone scenery of the eastern heights where shining mountain spires and towers are bordered by soft green lake-dotted pastures contrasts greatly with the rocky, rugged crag-enclosed deep cirques and glacier-spread clustered granite peaks at the heart of the range; while in places south of the frontier lie deep, wooded canyons out of which rise great multi-hued cliffs, totally unlike any other in the range. Every visit to the Pyrenees reveals new features, new splendour. It is an area to return to again and again.

To my mind, the biggest attraction of the Pyrenees for the walker is that they still have a wilderness quality gone from most of the mountains of southern Europe – at least below the snowline – a feeling of remoteness only occasionally sullied by the type of development that has ruined much of the Alps. Here there are still rarely-trodden trails leading into little-visited high cirques and along narrow ridges and it is still possible to walk for days on end without crossing a road or passing through a town. There are Alpine huts for those who prefer that type of accommodation but, if you rely on these, where you can travel will be very restricted and you will miss that sense of wonder at being part of the natural world that comes with spending your nights as well as days outside the confines of solid walls. To obtain the best from the Pyrenees, camp out far from the nearest sign of civilization; the range abounds with unbelievably beautiful potential campsites both high in the mountains and down in the valleys and may well be the best area for wilderness camping left in Europe. Be sure, though, that if you do camp out you leave no sign of your passing. Rugged the Pyrenees may be, but they are also highly vulnerable to damage from misuse and it is the responsibility of those who wander here to leave them untouched for those who come in the future and for the animals, birds and plants whose home this is.

Being lower than the Alps – the highest peak is Pico de Aneto (3,404 m/11,165 ft) – and with far fewer glaciers and permanent snowfields, the Pyrenees are also ideal mountains for the adventurous walker who likes to reach the summits. Where the sheer cliffs and steep, crevassed icefields of the highest peaks in the Alps make them solely the province of the trained mountaineer, most peaks in the Pyrenees can be reached by the keen scrambler with little or no technical skills and specialist equipment. Overall, this is a land for the walker and backpacker rather than the mountaineer.

The Pyrenees are quickly reached: by rail you can be in the heart of the mountains within twenty-four hours of leaving London. As they are well-mapped, too, it is easy to plan a trek at short notice. For these reasons they are an ideal destination for trips of a week or two as well as longer treks, and it is mainly for those who do not have the time, or perhaps the inclination, to wander in the mountains for months on end that this book is written. Some of the routes are linear ones, some are circular, 'tours' in the terminology of the region. I have, I hope, given enough details to help those planning walks of their own but my main aim has been to try to capture at least some of the joy and excitement of walking in these mountains; to convey in both words and pictures just what being in the Pyrenees is like with the aim of inspiring others to visit these mountains, with the hope that they remain relatively untouched and unspoilt.

For the long-distance walker, I have also included brief details of the two magnificent trails, the Grande Randonnée 10 and the Haute Randonnée Pyrénéene, that stretch from the Atlantic to the Mediterranean. These routes stride along the range, providing a wide overview of the diverse nature of the Pyrenees. However, to really experience the mountains you need to explore the details, venture into the hidden side-canyons and remote cirques, wander through the lake-filled wooded valleys and climb to the summits that rise above them. Every part of the range has its secrets and its own unique feel; to start to touch on this requires time and cannot be done on a long linear walk. To allow for such intimate delving into the heart of the mountains, I have included many suggestions for side-trips in the routes described here, some of which I have done myself, others that are still only dreams. By including these, the time taken for apparently short routes can suddenly stretch from a few days to a week, a fortnight, a month, a summer . . .

Chris Townsend

Through the High Mountains of the West:

Lescun to Gavarnie

> *This is a wild land, country of my choice,*
> *with harsh craggy mountain, moor ample and bare*
>
> Robert Graves
> *Rocky Acres*

Thirty-two hours, six trains, one boat and two buses after leaving home, Graham Huntington and I suddenly found ourselves alone in the crisp silent dark of a September Pyrenean night. All around lay the black shapes of the hills, concealing their secrets and intricate details. Wanting to reach the real start of our walk that night, we left the Aspe Valley where the final mini-bus had abruptly dumped us into the quiet immensity of the mountains, and followed a steeply switchbacking side road upwards for 400 metres (1,312ft) and six or so

kilometres (4 miles) to the outskirts of Lescun. The existence of this remote hamlet was marked only by a few yellow lights. A grassy bank provided a spot to lay out our sleeping bags under the stars for the first night of the trek, always an exciting moment, full of anticipation for camps to come and the adventure of travelling through glorious mountain scenery. Sometime during the night, though, rain swept in and had us sliding into bivvy bags and then at dawn hastily packing and dashing into the narrow streets and stone houses of

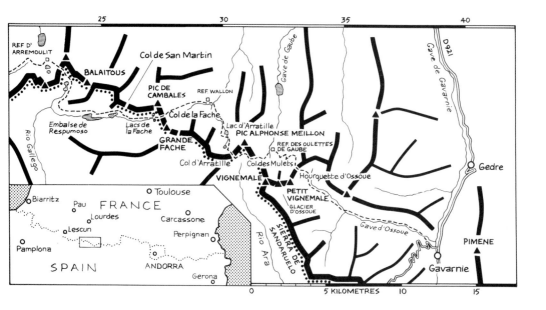

Lescun to search out a café for a lengthy two-hour breakfast and a final study of the maps. Outside the grey rain fell, blotting out the view.

Towering above the village of Lescun, the limestone peaks of the Cirque d'Ansabère along with 2,504m (8,213ft) Pic d'Anie a few kilometres to the north mark the start of the high mountains of the Pyrenees. To the west, the range dwindles slowly through the rolling green hills of the Basque country to the sandy beaches of the Atlantic. To the east lie the mountains and all the wonders they contain.

This first route starts in Lescun (public transport stops at the junction of the main Aspe valley and the turning for Lescun, so the walk up the road to the village has to be undertaken unless a taxi rather than the SCNF mini-bus is taken from Bedous to the north) and then stays close to the crest of the range, winding back and forth across the frontier along various alternatives of the High Level Route for nearly 110 kilometres (67 miles) before descending to the popular tourist centre of Gavarnie. Because it mostly stays high, there are no supply points along the route though there are a number of staffed huts. And because there is much climbing as well as distance involved, most walkers will want to take 8–10 days over it, not including any rest or side trip ones, so those not using the huts at all will need to start off with a fairly heavy pack containing all their food and fuel. Two weeks could easily be spent on the walk by those intending to climb peaks on the way or make side trips into inviting cirques or valleys or even just spend days lazing outside the tent. The walking is mostly on good paths and finding the way is easy. There is no need for ice axes or other technical equipment.

The way out of Lescun is signposted GR10 just by the small general store (useful for the purchase of last-minute supplies – fresh bread say or extra chocolate bars) and heads south-westwards along a metalled lane down and across the Gave d'Ansabère and then up beside the true right bank of the latter. Soon leaving the small fields for beech forest, the road becomes a rough track and the feeling of entering a mountain sanctuary grows as the first views of the soaring pinnacles of the Ansabère Aiguilles appear ahead. Then, after nine kilometres (5½ miles) and a 700m (2,296ft) climb, the path breaks out of the trees into the lower reaches of the Cirque d'Ansabère. Here lie the Cabanes d'Ansabère, rough stone huts wedged in between huge limestone boulders that are often occupied in the summer by shepherds tending the vast flocks of sheep that graze the hillsides round about and whose bells can be heard for miles around. Among the wind-stunted dwarf beech trees there are many grassy swards ideal for siting a tent and it was on one of these that, after making the climb in a cold gusty wind and swirling cloud that partly masked the peaks, we set up camp. Although only half a day's walk from Lescun, the cirque is a good overnight stopping place for those who have spent the previous day or so travelling to the mountains.

Another reason to camp here is to witness the dawn as the first rays of the sun light up the Grande and Petite Aiguilles (2,360m/7,740ft and 2,271m/7,448ft high respectively), turning the grey rock brilliant white, an impressive spectacle. We woke (after 11½ hours' sleep!) to clear skies and a frost on the tent and felt privileged to be able to lie in our sleeping bags over breakfast staring up at the magnificent rock spires as we waited for the sun to reach the tent. A closer look can be had by walking up into the cirque to the scree at the base of the pinnacles but this is as close as the walker can go, all ascent routes being technical rock climbs, though the neighbouring Pic d'Ansabère (2,377m/7,796ft) can be ascended

Shepherd's summer cabin high in the mountains.

by an easy scramble. I have not done this climb but the view of the Grande Aiguille from the summit is said to be magnificent.

The next stage of the walk involves climbing out of the Cirque d'Ansabère and crossing the frontier ridge at a shallow 1,991m (6,530ft) unnamed col to enter Spain for the first time. On the climb past the tiny and attractive Lac d'Ansabère, we saw hundreds of griffon vultures soaring overhead, a familiar though always exciting sight to walkers in these hills. Throughout the climb and from the ridge the karst limestone scenery is quite breath-taking. This is not an ascent to hurry. The view from the frontier shows wave after wave of flat-topped Spanish hills (the word mesa coming to mind) disappearing into a distant heat haze. A grassy descent leads down a spur to the beautiful waters of the Ibon de Acherito, a good place to fill up your water bottles as there are no guaranteed sources for some way to come. This is, after all, limestone country. From the lake a path descends a little, then turns north-eastwards through a shallow valley. The limestone pastureland crossed here is repete with the typical features of pot holes, sink holes, white banded outcrops and bright green turf, reminiscent of the landscapes of the Yorkshire Dales.

The frontier ridge is reached again and

the Pyrenees National Park is entered at the 1,942m (6,370ft) Col de Pau where we were surprised to walk immediately into a dense mist that had crept up unseen on the French side. From the col, a broader waymarked path leads round the French side of 2,105m (6,904ft) Pic de Burcq to rejoin the ridge again at the Col de Burcq and follow it to the Col de la Cuarde, from where it heads northeast into France and the 1,949m (6,393ft) Col de Saoubathou. I have no doubt this ridgecrest section can give superb views but it doesn't when clouds are rolling over it. All I noted was that the pale limestone was broken here by purple bands of other sedimentary rock and that there was much crumbling conglomerate. To make up for these missing vistas, however, the clouds cleared on the Col de Saoubathou to give an unexpected and spectacular view across the Aspe valley to the obvious dominant rock tower of the 2,885m (9,463ft) Pic du Midi d'Ossau.

Rounding the head of the darkly wooded straight line of the Belonce valley, the path next leads by way of some final switchbacks to the Refuge d'Arlet, a staffed hut essential to those seeking such accommodation but an intrusion abhorred by those who like the mountains untouched and untamed (my journal entry describes it as a 'horrible modern chalet-type hut'). Camping is restricted to certain overused areas in the vicinity of the hut but I cannot see why anyone would want to camp within sight of it as there are so many grand potential sites elsewhere. We passed the hut and the adjacent Lac d'Arlet and camped a kilometre or so further on by a tiny pool in the pastures of the Cirque de Banasse, the evening quiet broken only by the clanging of cow bells and the lowing of their wearers.

The path, clearly marked (on the map it is named the Tour de la Haute Vallée d'Aspe as well as the HRP), winds on to the 1,891m (6,202ft) Col de Lapachouaou from where

Graham Huntington climbing out of the Cirque d'Ansabère with the Ansabère Pinnacles in the background.

hunk of cheese weighing, at a guess, at least two kilos (4½ lb). This was rather more than we had wanted to spend or to carry, language difficulties having worked more in the favour of the shepherds than us. Still, it was very good cheese.

Soon after the cabane, the path plunges into the cool of the woods and descends, mostly through beech though occasionally through silver fir and black pine, to the grass and stream of the Pla d'Espelunguère. Then it climbs slightly back into the forest, and contours round the hillside before making a final descent to the Gave d'Aspe and the road to the Col du Somport and Spain. Above rises the broad and imposing Cirque d'Aspe. Those reliant on accommodation should leave the route here and seek some. The Refuge d'Arlet lies 10km (6 miles) and about some 4½ hours behind, and the next staffed hut, the Refuge d'Ayous, lies 14km (8½ miles) and maybe 5½ hours ahead. If you wish to stay in the vicinity, the choices are to walk or hitch-hike 2½km (1½ miles) up to the Col du Somport where there are hotels on the Spanish side, or 10km (6 miles) down the valley to Urdos where there is a hotel-restaurant.

Camping is technically forbidden here, as you are in the national park where it is only allowed an hour or more's walk from the road. Few backpackers will want to camp by the roadside anyway as there are many beautiful mountain sites to choose from on the route ahead. The official HRP route heads into the Cirque d'Aspe, then doubles back to cross the road, but most people will, I imagine, do as we did and follow the road up a short way to where a path marked 'Refuge Larry' leaves it at a hairpin bend. This heads north across a west-facing hillside, bare except for scrubby aromatic and very colourful Mediterranean plants. On hot, sunny days here lizards dart and myriads of bright red and blue winged grasshoppers whir incessantly. On a clear

there is a splendid view of the frontier peaks across the broad Aspe valley into which the route now starts to descend. Just before entering the trees of the Bois d'Espelunguère, the path passes the Cabane Grosse, inhabited on my visit by a few shepherds and a large pack of dogs, some of them large and magnificent Pyrenean Sheepdogs, that came racing across the path towards us. Luckily they were all very friendly. A crude painted sign outside displayed the single word: 'Fromage'. I patted the exuberant animals while Graham investigated the latter, emerging from the dark confines of the hut after a short while less eighty-eight francs but in possession of a huge afternoon this shadeless climb is hot work so it is worth taking frequent stops to look back to the massive ring of the Cirque d'Aspe. Afterwards, the drop into cool woods from the Col de Lazaque to cross two small streams is welcome.

A camp could be made here though the terrain is not ideal. A search away from the path might well reveal better sites, though I did not look too closely as we had already decided to push on to the Refuge Larry. This is reached after a climb out of the woods and a traverse of another open hillside. In all, it took Graham and I eight hours from the camp in the Cirque de Banasse. The Refuge Larry is a small unstaffed basic shelter provided by the national park with sleeping space for six or so people. There is a welcome water pipe outside, the only other facilities being mattresses to sleep on. Pitching a tent outside would be possible but when I was there all the flat ground had been trampled into dust and covered in dung by the huge flocks of sheep that forage in the area. Not wanting a tent that stank of sheep, we used the hut which we shared with three other walkers, a French pair and a solo Englishman.

By dawn I wished I had chosen the smell of sheep as the hut was hot and stuffy, the overnight temperatures not dropping below

Village of Lescun on the west bank of the Aspe Valley.

15

Graham Huntington outside the tiny Refuge de Larry.

15°C (59°F). Beyond the refuge the path climbs up to the 2,130m (6,986ft) Col du Larry, where the GR10 joins the HRP from the north, and shortly afterwards the 2,185m (7,167ft) Col d'Ayous from where there is a magnificent view over the Bious valley to the now much nearer Pic du Midi d'Ossau. Perhaps a more welcome sight for any hut-to-hut trekker who has walked from the Refuge d'Arlet in one go is seen from the path as you descend from the pass of the Refuge d'Ayous – another modern PNP hut. Camping is forbidden near this hut. But again, who would want to?

The 1:25,000 Série Bleue map marks the HRP/GR10 beyond the hut as descending eastwards into the Bious valley, then climbing back up beside the Gave de Bious. A much more scenic route, though, and the one I recommend is that described as the HRP in both the Veron and Reynolds trail guides. This runs south above Lac Bersau before turning east to Lac Casterau, a beautiful little lake nestling under the huge rock wall of the south face of 2,227m (7,304ft) Pic Casterau. This path gives several superb views of the Pic du Midi d'Ossau towering above the woods and pastures of the Bious valley, while the many disappearing streams and limestone and marble 'sinks' in the area add to the interest. Eventually the path descends into the head of the Bious valley, a good place for a rest or even a camp, then ascends steep grassy slopes to pastureland and the Lac de Peygeret. Beyond this pretty lake the walk becomes quite tough for the first time as a huge boulder field has to be negotiated. Cairns mark the way but care and good balance plus a fair amount of energy are required to cross the blocks of rock to the 2,300m (7,544ft) Col de Peygeret from where there is an overpowering view of the great granite hulk of the Pic du Midi d'Ossau, one of the most striking individual peaks of the Pyrenees. When you have recovered from this, the big peaks to come, among them the Balaitous and the Vingemale, can be seen away to the east. Below the pass lies the CAF Refuge de Pombie on the banks of the Lac de Pombie, a popular hut as it is the base for climbs on the Pic du Midi. Camping is permitted around the hut, but only for periods of less than forty-eight hours. Unless you need the hut facilities there is no real need for you to camp close by, however.

If you want to climb the Pic du Midi, either the Pombie hut or a camp in this area is the best place for a base. I have not climbed the peak – the easiest route up which involves some steep scrambling but is not technically difficult – mainly because safety helmets are recommended as there is a danger of stones being knocked down by other parties (this being a popular ascent) and I have not wanted to lug a helmet so far just for this climb. One day I will do so as it is a shame to pass by such a fine peak.

Just below the Col de Peygeret lie two small lakes and some grassy shelves. The latter make an excellent place to spend the night as the impressive south face of the Pic du Midi rises directly above. The weather being calm and the sky cloudless, Graham and I bivvied out here watching the walls of the great mountain above darkening as the sun set and listening to the calls of the last rock climbers as they hurried to be off the face before night fell. I set up my little stove next to my sleeping bag, lit it, put on a pan of water for a hot drink and lay back to enjoy the peace of dusk. By 9.15 p.m. the sky was brilliant with stars and the temperature 8°C (46°F). I slept naked and

did not bother using the bivvy bag.

Our tranquil night was abruptly disturbed at dawn. I had woken at 2.30 a.m. to see light clouds drifting overhead. By 7 a.m. black, denser clouds were pouring in over the shoulder of the Pic du Midi and we were gulping down breakfast. Soon after 8 a.m., thunder, heavy rain and strong winds had us donning waterproofs and packing hastily. The storm chased us down past the Pombie hut and a dozen tents into the rich beech woods of the Brousset valley where the rain finally stopped and the sun came out, causing the wet vegetation to steam. Near where the HRP crosses the road in the valley, which runs into Spain over the Col du Pourtalet, refreshments are available at the Cabane du Caillous de Soques, a ramshackle bar-restaurant. We had some rather unpleasant lukewarm coffee here, the only place in the Pyrenees where I have ever been disappointed in the quality of what I have been served. This put us off ordering any food, but we had still rather a lot of the Cabane Grosse cheese to eat.

From the road there is a long haul up the Arrious valley, mitigated by views back to the Pic du Midi d'Ossau, to the 2,259m (7,409ft) Col d'Arrious. There is a choice of paths here, both leading to the staffed Refuge d'Arremoulit. We took the left-hand (north-east) branch descending slightly to the Lac d'Artouste, which seemed to be holding back a wall of cloud that filled the valley below. From the lake, the steep zigzags lead up to the small (30-bed) CAF refuge. This is the base for the easiest route up the Balaitous, another peak I have not climbed, for which rope, ice axe and safety helmet are recommended.

At the refuge there is another choice of route, this one determining where you will be for the next day or two. The northerly route (the HRP proper, if there is such a thing) goes by way of the Col du Palas and Port du Lavedan round the rugged north side of the

Balaitous to the Refuge de Larribet, and then via the Col de Cambales to the Refuge Wallon in the Marcadau region. The southerly Spanish alternative descends from the Col du Palas to the Lacs d'Arriel and then passes the dammed Respumoso lake before returning to France and arriving at the Refuge Wallon by the Col de la Fache. Both the Veron and Reynolds trail guides give warnings about the northerly route ('not recommended to trekkers unaccustomed to the high mountains' and 'for experienced mountain trekkers only').

Owing to the rather embarrassing fact that neither of us had a map that covered the northern route because of confusion in our planning (each thought the other was bringing it) and the fact that the weather was still unsettled with dark clouds whipping overhead, Graham and I opted for the southern alternative. So, not yet having been back with a map to find out, I cannot tell you what the northern route is like, but I can say that the southern one is not as easy as the trail guides make out.

Beyond the Arremoulit hut lies a desolate

Trail sign in the Aspe Valley.

granite landscape dotted with cold pools and lakes. We picked our way across this and then, owing to the lack of a map, climbed to the wrong pass, the Col d'Arremoulit rather than the Col du Palas (we later met a couple who had crossed the right col; they described the descent from it on steep scree above cliffs as difficult so perhaps for the southern route our 'error' is the best way). From the Col d'Arremoulit we had an awe-inspiring view of the steep rock, ice and snow slopes of the Balaitous, at 3,146m (10,319ft) the most westerly of the 3,000 metre peaks, and its surrounding peaks. A steep descent on a narrow path leads directly down to the Lacs d'Arriel where we camped on the narrow strip of flat ground between these lakes and the broken rock walls that tower above on every side. Marmots called from the boulder fields. They were imported to the Pyrenees from the Alps many years ago since when they have colonized the area with great success.

In keeping with the wild and grim terrain, the night was stormy and we woke to wind, rain and low clouds, glad that we had not attempted the northern route. The route south leads down past a number of hemmed-in lakes and abandoned dams and buildings. Narrow passages beside roaring streams under high rock walls connect the lakes, passages that we felt could easily become impassable after heavy rain or spring snowmelt, the narrow path being only inches from and above the water. Once past the last lake, a good path leads eastwards away from the Arriel stream and contours across the hillside high above the Rio Aguas Limpias to the dammed Respumoso lake. Among the ruins at the west end of this reservoir lies a fairly intact church which is clearly used as a shelter by walkers and climbers.

We continued on along the north shore of the lake to an abandoned dam at the Campo Plano and then up a narrow rock-filled valley to the tiny Lacs de la Fache that lie below the Col de la Fache. Large snow patches filled much of this boulder-strewn miniature cirque when we were there, even though it was mid-September. One large, steeply sloping one that ended abruptly above deep water proved impassable in lightweight flexible walking boots. Ice axes were needed too because of the hardness of the snow, but being without them we found a way round the far side of the lake before making the final climb to the 2,664m (8,738ft) col. Earlier in the season there can be enough snow to make ice axes and even crampons necessary.

The summits still being in cloud, as they had been all day, we did not ascend the Grande Fache (3,005m/9,865ft) itself, an obvious option for anyone walking this route in good weather as it is only a half-hour climb up a good path from the pass. The descent is initially in a fairly steep stony valley but a good national park path is soon picked up that leads down to the large staffed Refuge Wallon. We camped on the Pla de Loubosso a couple of kilometres before the hut in green grassy surroundings and by a pleasant stream.

Sadly the tops were still cloud-capped the next morning but the views here are reputedly excellent. There were many people and a couple of tents outside the Refuge Wallon as we passed by to start the long ascent of the Gave d'Arratille valley to the 2,528m (8,292ft) Col d'Arratille, a pleasant climb through woods and then rocky lake-filled basins. From this col anyone bored with the high country and wanting to spend time in the beautiful canyons (and hot sunny weather) of the Spanish side could descend to the tempting-looking woods below and follow the winding Rio Ara down to the Ordesa Canyon to make a link with the route described in the third chapter.

Those aiming for Gavarnie, as we were, will make this dip into Spain a short one and cut

across the scree under the Pic Alphonse Meillon to 2,591m (8,498ft) Col de Mulets. Veron suggests dropping down to the grass seen below and then climbing back up to the col but I can see no point in doing this. Our trek between the two passes only took forty minutes.

From the Col des Mulets the path drops steeply down a narrow valley to the flat plain of the Oulettes du Vingemale and the CAF Refuge des Oulettes de Gaubes. At the head of the long swampy plain lies the Glacier des Oulettes and the great north face of the 3,298m (10,817ft) Vingemale, perhaps the most impressive peak in the Pyrenees, a view certainly held by its greatest devotee, Count Henry Russell. He climbed the mountain thirty-three times and spent one night in August 1880 on the summit in a shallow grave excavated there for the purpose. Nine years later, in honour of his obsession, the Syndicat of the valley of Barèges leased the four summits of the mountain to him at a fee of one franc a year. A number of grottoes built under Russell's direction exist on the mountain.

The splendid vista of the north face of the Vingemale, its summit wreathed in clouds which dissolved and reformed around the glaciers and icefalls, took most of the sting out of the switchbacking ascent to the 2,734m (8,968ft) Hourquette d'Ossue. An hour's easy climb south of the pass lies the 3,032m (9,945ft) Petit Vingemale, a recommended ascent in clear weather. Cloud still hiding the peaks, we contented ourselves with the view from the pass and then descended to the Refuge Bayssellance, a CAF hut that is the best base for an ascent of the Vingemale. The standard route, although technically easy, involves climbing the crevassed Ossue glacier, so rope, crampons and ice axe are needed.

The continuing descent from the Refuge Bayssellance is on a spectacular path that

Graham Huntington starting the descent from the Col de la Fache.

winds narrowly down scree slopes and across bits of old hard-packed snow and ice above a deep ravine to the flat glacial moraine of the Oulettes d'Ossau. Here there are many potential camp sites, one of which we used, though it is only two hours' walk down the road at the far end of the dammed Ossau lake to Gavarnie. We arrived there the .next morning on our eighth day out, to be overwhelmed by the smell and noise of the donkeys and horses used to take tourists to see the Cirque de Gavarnie, a tradition dating back to the last century, and the presence of vast hordes (or so it seems after a week in the solitude of the mountains) of people. Gavarnie is a tourist centre *par excellence* with all that implies. It does have one grocery store,

though, and a pleasant basic camp site on its southern edge plus several good restaurants, very welcome after the days of dehydrated meals.

An alternative to the final road walk would be to use the GR10 which joins the HRP again at the Refuge des Oulettes de Gaubes and which traverses the hillside high above the road before dropping down into Gavarnie. The road is quiet and quick, however, so those thinking, as we were, of three-course meals will undoubtably use it. The HRP itself climbs back into the mountains from the Oulettes d'Ossau and heads for the Sarradet hut on the edge of the Cirque de Gavarnie. This is the way for walkers using huts to go if they wish to continue their journey. Those

ROUTE

Distance		Place	Elevation	
[km]	[miles]		[metres]	[feet]
0.0	0.0	Lescun	.880	2,886
5.0	3.0	Pont Lamareich	960	3,149
9.0	5.5	Cabanes de Ansabère	1,560	5,117
11.0	7.0	frontier ridge	1,991	6,530
17.0	10.5	Col de Pau	1,942	6,370
21.0	13.0	Col de Saoubathou	1,949	6,393
24.0	15.0	Refuge d'Arlet	2,000	6,560
27.0	17.0	Col de Lapachouaou	1,891	6,202
34.0	21.0	Gave d'Aspe	1,320	4,330
45.0	28.0	Refuge de Larry	1,750	5,740
48.0	30.0	Refuge d'Ayous	1,982	6,501
57.0	35.5	Refuge de Pombie	2,031	6,662
62.0	38.5	Cabane de Caillou de Soques	1,392	4,566
68.0	42.0	Refuge d'Arremoulit	2,305	7,560
69.0	43.0	Col du Palas	2,515	8,249
75.0	46.5	Respumoso dam	2,121	6,957
80.0	49.5	Col de la Fache	2,664	8,738
84.0	52.0	Refuge Wallon	1,865	6,117
89.0	55.0	Col d'Arratille	2,528	8,292
91.0	56.5	Col des Mulets	2,591	8,498
92.5	57.5	Refuge des Oulettes de Gaube	2,151	7,055
95.0	59.0	Hourquette d'Ossau	2,734	8,968
95.75	59.5	Refuge Baysellance	2,651	8,695
100.75	62.5	Ossau dam	1,834	6,016
108.75	67.5	Gavarnie	1,375	4,510

who set off from Lescun with camping gear and all their food will want to restock in Gavarnie, however, and probably have a day off there even if they are walking further, so it seems a suitable place to end this venture into the high mountains of the western Pyrenees.

The route is mostly along the High Level Route or an alternative and the general direction is east. It starts in Lescun where a sign on the edge of the village points up a lane to the Cirque d'Ansabère. After a few kilometres, this lane crosses the Pont Lamareich and becomes an unmetalled track, climbing through beech woods above the right bank of the Gave d'Ansabère eventually to emerge from the trees in the Cirque d'Ansabère, just below the rough shelters of the Cabanes de Ansabère. Here the route swings to the south to climb out of the cirque and cross the frontier at an unnamed pass. Now in Spain, the path drops down to the Ibon de Acherito and then turns eastwards to cross high-level limestone pastures to the frontier again at Col de Pau. From this col, the HRP stays on or near the frontier until the Col de la Cuarde where it swings north-eastwards to the Col de Saoubathou then south-east to the Refuge d'Arlet.

The next col is Lapachouaou, reached after a traverse round the Cirque de Banasse. Now the route starts on a long circuit round the head of the Aspe valley involving a long wooded descent to the road in the valley, then an equally long north-eastwards rising traverse to the tiny unstaffed Refuge de Larry. Trending eastwards now, the path crosses the Col d'Ayous and descends to Lac Gentau and the Refuge d'Ayous, then turns south briefly to pass Lac Bersau and back east again past Lac Casterau to descend into the Bious valley. A long climb then leads to the Col de Peyreget and a shorter descent to the Refuge de Pombie under the walls of the Pic du Midi d'Ossau.

The descent continues down into the Brousset valley where the path crosses another road at the bar-restaurant of Soques.

Next comes a long climb beside the Arrious stream to the Col d'Arrious and, after a short drop to Lac d'Artouste and a reascent, the Refuge d'Arremoulit. Rough stony slopes then lead to the Col d'Arremoulit or Col de Palas, from either of which a path leads down into Spain and to the Arriel lakes and then round a broad shoulder to the Respumoso reservoir and the Campo Plano, from where an ascent leads to the Col de la Fache and a return to France. Once over the col, the path leads down to the Refuge Wallon and then straight back up to the frontier again at the Col d'Arratile. A brief traverse across the Spanish screes to the south of the Pic Alphonse Meillon leads to the Col des Mulets and a final re-entry into France. A short descent leads to the Refuge des Oulettes de Gaube under the great north face of the Vingemale. Switchbacking upwards, the path then climbs to the highest point of the route at the Hourquette d'Ossoue from where the final descent leads past the Refuge de Baysellence to the Ossau dam and road D128 to Gavarnie.

MAPS

IGN Série Bleu 1:25,000:1547 ouest Accous, 1547 est Laruns, 1648 est Vignemale, 1748 ouest Gavarnie. IGN Carte de Randonnées 1:50,000 No. 3 Bearn, No. 4 Bigorre.

TRAIL GUIDES

Reynolds, Kev, *Walks and Climbs in the Pyrenees* (Cicerone Press)
Veron, Georges, *Pyrenees High Level Route* (Gaston West Col)

A Tour of the Ordesa Canyon

> Miles which do not feed the senses and nourish the spirit are just empty statistics. Distance is in a sense meaningless. It is the journey through time and nature that matters.
>
> Mike Cudahy
> **Wild Trails to Far Horizons**

The Ordesa Canyon is only a small place, barely more than 10km (6 miles) long. You can walk up and down it in half a day. But to do so would be to miss virtually everything this unique marvel has to offer. Carved out of the rock by the Rio Arazas as it powers down from 3,355m (11,004ft) Monte Perdido, the third highest in the range, the Ordesa Canyon is a wonderland, a gem of natural beauty for which no superlatives are adequate. Above the magnificent forests of beech, pine and silver fir that line the banks of the Arazas, massive castellated tiers of multi-hued yellow, purple and red banded limestone climb 1,000m (3,280ft) into the sky. These glorious cliffs with their fantastic buttresses line the canyon on both sides throughout its length, forcing the eye ever upwards.

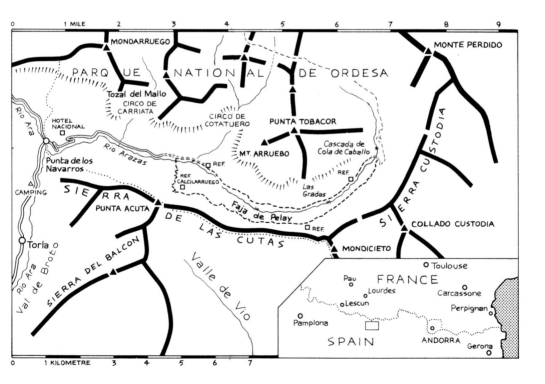

The walls of Ordesa seen from the west.

That this canyon is unique was recognized as long ago as 1917 when the 5,450 acre Parque Nacional de Ordesa was created, a designation that has thankfully prevented the development of the easily accessible upper reaches of Arazas. A road penetrates the first 4km (2½ miles) of the canyon past the Parador state hotel to a car park, gift shop and restaurant, beyond which footpaths are the only mark of humanity. To help keep it pristine camping is not allowed in the park below the 2,000m (6,560ft) mark, which means not in the canyon itself.

Ordesa can be reached on foot from the north by a variety of routes, two of which – from Gavarnie via the Port de Gavarnie and the valley of the Rio Ara and from Gavarnie via the Brèche de Roland, a huge gash in the cliffs of the Cirque de Gavarnie – can be

linked to form a circular walk as described in the next chapter. By road the best way is over the Col du Pourtalet south of Laruns in France and then via Sallent and Biescas to the village of Torla, 6km (3½ miles) south of the mouth of the canyon. The distance from the col is 60km (37 miles).

Torla is an attractive medieval village with good views of the cliffs at the mouth of Ordesa. The central area is relatively unspoilt but new hotels and apartments are being built to the north, towards Ordesa, creating something of a modern ribbon-development sprawl. As well as indoor accommodation, Torla also has a camp site (behind the Hotel Ordesa) but unfortunately it is too far (10km/6 miles) from the roadhead in the canyon to be a convenient base for those on foot. There are also a number of organized camp sites north of the canyon's entrance in the Ara valley but, again, these are a little too far to be of much use except as overnight stopping places.

The only mountain hut is the staffed Refugio de Goriz, run by the Federacion Espanola de Montanismo, on the slopes of Monte Perdido above the head of the canyon. This is perhaps the best base for exploration of the canyon if only because, by being far from the road, it has the feel of wilderness, something Torla's hotels and regimented camp site, with its dusty square pitches and neat privet hedges, lack. Camping is permitted around the hut which, although in the national park, lies above the 2,000m contour line. The Reynolds guide says that camping in the vicinity of the Goriz hut is 'difficult' but I have seen twenty or more tents spread out along the grassy terraces near the hut on what look to be perfectly adequate and highly scenic, if somewhat exposed, sites. There are also superb potential pitches higher up the Circo de Goriz, two of which I have used and would recommend. All provide easier access to the canyon than Torla.

Whether you use Torla or the Goriz area as a base, I would recommend devoting at least a complete day to wandering in the Ordesa Canyon. The circular day walk described here could easily be repeated on successive days without losing any of its impact. Indeed, I spent two days on it, walking up the canyon from Torla to camp in the Circo de Goriz one day and then trekking the length of the Faja de Pelay twice on the same day two days later (In between I climbed Monte Perdido, but that story belongs to another chapter. One advantage of a base high in the mountains to the east of the canyon is that it opens up a number of possibilities for an extended stay). The whole round trip is only 21km (13 miles), yet if it takes you less than all day you are hurrying. And Ordesa is not a place to hurry but a place to take in slowly, to savour, a

place to stop almost between steps to absorb the atmosphere and gaze in awe at the unbelievable rock architecture and the almost unbearable beauty of the forest.

Assuming an approach from Torla and the west, as we have to start somewhere, the walk begins at the car park for those with transport. Although the traffic can be a nuisance, however, the walk from Torla allows the cliffs at the entrance of the canyon to unfold slowly, particularly dramatic being those of 2,615m (8,577ft) Mondarruego to the north, and gives a less abrupt introduction to the splendours of the canyon. At the Puente de Navarros the road crosses the Rio Ara, enters the national park and switchbacks up past the Hotel Nacional Parador de Ordesa into the wide, flat lower canyon and through thick mature forest to the car park and restaurant. For those walking this section there are a number of paths that shortcut some of the hairpin bends and also keep you away from the cars. From the car park there ensues a magical walk through splendid scenery with the Rio Arazas tumbling down in a series of cascades through the heart of the forest. The vast rock walls rise above, often seen temptingly through gaps in the trees and at times more clearly from the meadows, flower-filled in spring, that break up the forest. Then there is the light! In sunshine the canyon walls glow, vibrant with colour, the river sparkles and the trees glisten as their leaves ripple in the breeze, reflecting the sun's rays. This combination of cliff, forest and river; rock, leaf and water seems as near to perfection as can be imagined.

From the car park a wide path heads off through the shrubbery and into the forest, mostly staying well away from the Arazas but soon crossing the Cotatuero stream (the path branching left just before the stream leads into the Circo de Cotatuero). Whenever the path crosses a meadow, which it does several times, views of the canyon walls suddenly open up.

Las Gradas, a series of small cascades near the head of the canyon.

Back towards the mouth of the canyon can be seen the sheer rock tower of the Tozal del Mallo whose profile Kev Reynolds describes as 'hallucinatory'. Its 400m (1,312ft) south face was first climbed in 1957 and now boasts a number of routes, none of them remotely easy. North of the path here is the huge Circo de Cotatuero up whose retaining walls an easy, if exposed, peg-aided climb (Alpine grade AD) can be made. No technical equipment is needed, just a good head for heights. Making up the east wall of the cirque is the huge La Fraucata face of 2,751m (9,023ft) Monte Arruebo which can be seen soaring above the forest, while lining the canyon to the south is the flat-topped Sierra de las Cutas.

After a few wondrous kilometres, the path starts to climb, giving many superb views over

The walls of Mondarruego from the east.

The northern cliffs of Ordesa from the Faja de Pelay.

the lower canyon as well as some of the cascades on the Arazas below. The initial switchbacking climb is short, soon leaving the forest for the flat pastureland of the upper canyon where the Arazas tumbles down the rocky steps in a series of picturesque cascades known as Las Gradas. The path, always clear, ascends the rocks next to these miniature waterfalls and their attendant dwarf conifers into a longer stretch of meadows, at the far end of which is the Circo de Soasco and the end of the canyon. Tumbling into the cirque is the Cascada de Cola de Caballo, above which rises the bare rock and scree of Monte Perdido.

Just before the waterfall the path starts to climb the right wall of the valley, dividing almost immediately into the branch leading to the Refugio de Goriz, which lies 3km (2 miles)

to the north, and the branch heading back west into the canyon. It is the latter we want. Climbing gently but steadily, the path takes the walker on to the broad terrace of the Faja de Pelay which traverses the south wall of the canyon at around the 1,900m contour line and provides spectacular views down into the depths of the canyon where the thin black line of the Arazas cuts through the dark swathe of the forest, while across the huge empty space at one's feet can be seen the stupendous cliffs of the north canyon wall tailing off above to the rather dull-looking summits of Punta Tobaco (2,780m/9,118ft) and Monte Arruebo. As one progresses along the terrace, views open out into the Circo de Cotatuero and beyond it the back of the Cirque de Gavarnie with the Brèche de Roland clearly identifiable. Closer to hand, there are wild flowers, gnarled black pines and, if you are lucky, close views of some of the isards, the chamois of the Pyrenees, that live on these cliffs. We say many of these delicate yet nimble creatures, a type of primitive goat-antelope, including one that stared down at us for long moments from only metres away before bounding off up the scree.

After 8km (5 miles) or so a tiny shelter with the grand name of the Refugio y Mirador de Calcilarruego o de la Proa marks the end of the high level walk. Just before this shelter, the path starts steeply down the hillside, dropping in tight switchbacks for 600m (1,968ft) to the canyon floor and a wooden footbridge over the Arazas beyond which lies the car park.

There are no other walks in the Ordesa Canyon apart from that into the Circo de Cotatuero, but only a few kilometres to the east lies the hidden and little-known Vallée de Ansiclo, a narrow gorge reputedly well worth a visit by those whose desire to wander canyon depths rather than mountain heights has been stirred by Ordesa. Anisclo can be visited in a day from the Refugio de Goriz via the Barranco de la Pardina or the Barranco Arrablo. Next time I am in the area I intend doing so.

ROUTE

Distance		Place	Elevation	
[km]	[miles]		[metres]	[feet]
0.0	0.0	Roadhead	1,360	4,461
7.0	4.5	Las Gradas	1,660	5,445
10.0	6.0	Cascada de Cola de Caballo	1,760	5,773
20.0	12.5	Refugio y Mirador	1,900	6,232
21.0	13.0	Roadhead	1,360	4,461

The route is simple: follow the path along the valley floor to the Circo de Soasco, then back along the Faja de Pelay before descending steeply back to the Arazas.

TRAIL GUIDE

Kev Reynolds, *Walks and Climbs in the Pyrenees* (Circerone Press)

MAPS

Editorial Alpina 1:40,000 Valle de Ordesa: IGN Carte de Randonnées 1:50,000 No. 4 Bigorre.

A Tour of Gavarnie:
Monte Perdido and the Brèche de Roland

> *The majesty of hills is not a matter of mere height and size; it is what we find among them – beauty, health, exercise, friends and fresh air.*
>
>

Frank Smythe
The Adventures of a Mountaineer

Gavarnie is the one place that no visitor to the Pyrenees can avoid for long. To many tourists, perhaps 'doing' Europe in a two-week whirlwind coach tour, it is the Pyrenees. I remember sitting at a table outside a café in the village centre when a coach rolled up bearing British number plates and disgorged a mass of people, most of whom disappeared into the café, though a few of the more adventurous did wander off to browse in the gift shops. Within an hour they all piled back on board and were driven off north, their visit to the Pyrenees over. None had seen the huge cirque that lies just a few kilometres further south and which first brought tourists here. Most visitors do, though, make the pilgrimage, usually on the backs of Gavarnie's myriad horses and donkeys, to the foot of the great walls of the Cirque de Gavarnie that stretch 1,300m (4,254ft) into the sky.

For the walker, Gavarnie has far more to offer than the cirque, though that should not be missed, early morning or late evening being the best times for the short walk to the base of the great tiers of rock as then the hordes are absent and the path is free of animals. It is one of the few villages close enough to the mountains to make a viable base and the only one that gives access to many different areas. There are many possibilities for day treks, one of which, the ascent of 2,801m (9,187ft) Pimène, is given as an addenda to the rather longer walk described here. Day tours are

limited by the need to return to base, however, and also remove the pleasure of nights spent in remote camps high in the hills.

This walk takes in several of the main attractions of the Gavarnie region on both the French and Spanish sides of the frontier and features a great diversity of scenery, from the beautiful woods and deep canyons of the Rio Ara and the Ordesa Canyon to the stark rock and scree of Monte Perdido, the Brèche de Roland and Le Taillon. The basic route is quite short, though there is a great deal of ascent; it could be walked in three days (probably in two by the strong walker) if the ascent of Perdido were omitted. I recommend allowing five or more days, though, in order to have time to absorb the atmosphere of the mountains and gain more than a fleeting impression of their grandeur. It is possible to do the trek using accommodation every night as two staffed refuges (Sarradet and Goriz) lie on the route, and the guest houses and hotels of Torla are nearby. Although the opportunities for wilderness camping are not as great as on other treks, the use of a tent will, as always, enable the walker to experience the mountains in all their aspects and not just under the midday sun. No special gear is needed, though an ice axe and crampons could be useful for the ascent of Perdido until late in the season. I have assumed a start in Gavarnie but those with a vehicle may wish to drive to the Port de Gavarnie and park there,

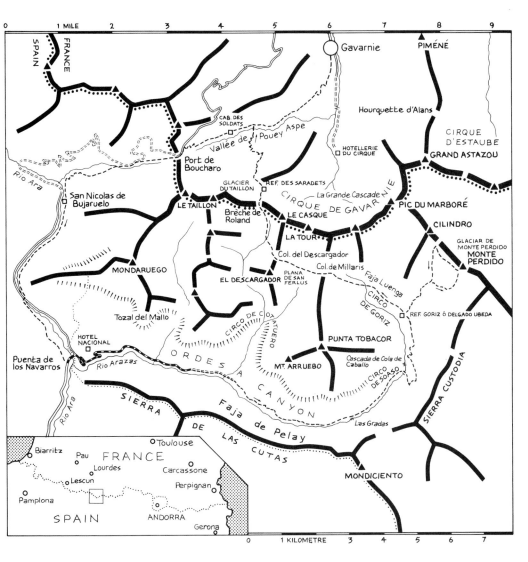

shortening the walk a little and cutting out the initial 900m (2,952ft) climb.

The walk starts in the centre of Gavarnie by the church, from where a path leads off towards the cirque. Soon it switchbacks up the side of the valley, with good views over the fields to the solitary summit of Pimène on the far side, and then curves above the fast tumbling waters of the Gave des Tourettes and enters the long Vallée de Pouey Aspe. Here,

on my first visit, an early season snowstorm cut short an attempt to climb up to the Brèche de Roland, and Graham Huntington and I spent a whole day in the tent as the blizzard raged outside. With no ice axes and only light bendy footwear, we viewed the snow-plastered slopes above the valley with dismay the next day before reluctantly heading back into Gavarnie. On my second visit, though, with Alain Kahan and Mark Edgington, the last clouds of a day-long downpour (during which we stayed in the cafés and restaurants of Gavarnie) were clearing from the peaks of the cirque, and the climb into the Vallée de Pouey Aspe was hot work though amply rewarded by the views.

The ascent eases in the valley itself, a beautiful place with many potential campsites and also the small single-roomed and rather dark and gloomy Cabane des Soldats, which could be useful refuge in bad weather. As the head of the valley is approached, the slopes start to steepen and the line of the road from Gavarnie up the Vallée des Especieres to the north can be seen cutting across the hillside above. A final short clamber over boulders, most of it debris from when the road was built, leads to the large flattened area on the Port de Gavarnie (Port de Boucharo on many maps)

where cars can be left. The road stops here, on the frontier ridge, as the Spanish section has never been built, although the intended line of it appears on several maps. Instead, a path, steep and rough in places but always clear, leads down from the stony wastes of the pass through the Lapazosa valley to the colourful mixed woodland and pale cliffs of the Rio Ara valley over 900m (2,952ft) below. It is a pleasant descent, marred only by the electricity pylons that march up the hillside close by.

In the valley bottom, refreshments and a campsite are available at San Nicolas de Bujaruelo which lies across the ancient and picturesque stone bridge of the same name. Both the Reynolds and Battagel trail guides give the route as continuing along the road down the valley but, if you want to avoid most of the tarmac and traffic, do not cross the

Alain Kahan on the GR11 path beside the Rio Ara.

bridge but instead take the path, waymarked GR11, that runs above the east bank of the river. This path runs through beautiful mature silver fir and beech forest with boxwood, holly, whitebeam, elder, birch and willow understory. Occasionally you break out of the cool confines of the trees into bright meadows from where high, thin waterfalls can be seen tumbling down the cliffs on either side of the valley, while by one's side the Ara rushes past over a series of rapids. Whether camping is allowed in these woods I do not know but there are many secluded potential sites. The path joins the road where the latter crosses the river some 2.5km (1½ miles) from the entrance to the Ordesa Canyon National Park, the great rock walls of which soon come into view stretching away to the north, an awe-inspiring sight. At the Puente de los Navarros, a bridge across the river, the road splits, one branch climbing up into the canyon, the other continuing down the Ara valley.

Those with plenty of time and stamina may want to continue through the canyon to stay in or camp near the Goriz refuge. Most people, however, knowing that there is no-where to stay or camp for another 17km (this being forbidden in the national park below the 2,000m (6,560ft) contour line which means anywhere in the canyon itself) will want to find somewhere to stay hereabouts, 20km (12½ miles) already having been walked (a camp in the Pouey Aspe or a start from the Port de Gavarnie would, of course, shorten this distance and make reaching the Goriz hut in a day more feasible). It is possible to camp near the Ara here, preparatory to the walk up the canyon, though again whether this is officially permitted or not I do not know. The alternative is to walk 4km (2½ miles) down the road to the village of Torla where there is a dusty and regimented but perfectly adequate campsite behind the large Hotel Ordesa and a selection of hotels and guest houses plus, of course, restaurants and food stores.

From the Los Navarros bridge the route passes through the Ordesa Canyon, a glorious walk described in detail in the previous chapter. Initially it involves a slog up the road, a hot steep climb mitigated by the views. There are paths short-cutting some of the hairpin bends the road makes. I would recommend walking this road from Torla, if that is where you have spent the night, early in the morning before the tourist traffic starts to build up. Once the large car park at the roadhead is reached, trail travel is resumed and a good path taken through the forest in the valley bottom. The cliff scenery here is truly magnificent. At the head of the canyon the path climbs steeply out of the Circo de Soasco, then traverses the rocky terraces that make up the lower slopes of Monte Perdido to the Refuge de Goriz. Campsites can be found around the hut and also further to the north-west in the Circo de Goriz. We camped by a small waterfall just below but out of sight of the hut, a camp that we moved a few kilometres to the north a day later to a flat open expanse through which a stream flows below the small cliffs of the Faja Luenga. Late in the evening I climbed up the lower slopes of Punta Tabacor to watch Monte Perdido turn golden in the last sunlight of the day. After dark, a line of lights marked the last walkers heading for the hut under the starry sky. It was a delight to be out there in the freedom of the wilderness after the neat rows of tent squares and clipped hedges of the too-well-ordered campsite in Torla where we had spent the previous night.

The limestone landscape hereabouts is stark and arid but has a desolate and wild beauty. It is certainly worth spending some time explor- ing the area even if you are not intent on climbing Monte Perdido. The ascent of this, at 3,355m (11,005ft), the third highest peak in the Pyrenees, is easy and well worth while, however. It is called the Lost Mountain because from the north it is blocked from view by the frontier peaks and can only be seen from a few points. From the south, however, it dominates the view and it is the peaks north of the border that are 'lost'. Early exploration of the range was from France, however, hence the name. It was first climbed by two French mountain guides, Laurens and Rondau, plus a Spanish shepherd, in 1802.

The easiest and most popular route, the 'voie normale', is the one that starts at the Goriz hut. Cairns and traces of path mark the way up a series of steepening grass terraces and bands of rock. At one point where the path traverses a narrow ledge above a waterfall, Mark and I (Alain, not a mountain climber, having stayed below to wander the lower slopes in search of interesting plants) left the standard route (in part, it must be admitted, because I did not fancy making the few exposed steps on slippery rock in the running shoes I was wearing, not the ideal footwear for this climb) and crossed the steep scree south of the peak to below a steep wall breached at one point by a 10m (33ft) gully up which we scrambled. This is far more exposed than the standard route but leads to an easy walk over loose rock to the summit, marked by a triangulation point and a small iron cross. The view is superb. To the north can be seen the huge east wall of 3,328m (10,916ft) Cilindro and the Cirque de Gavarnie peaks with the distant glacier-slashed bulk of the Vingemale further round to the west. South is the dark gash of the little-known Anisclo canyon, while to the south-east the perfect curve of Monte Arruebo drops away to become the shadowed upper reaches of the Ordesa Canyon.

Even in late September the summit was snow-covered, as was the descent gully in which our long staffs proved more use than the ice axes others were using. Earlier in the season, though, the latter plus crampons may

The Goriz hut.

well be needed. Soon after the start of the descent it is possible to take a few steps east of the path and peer down to the contorted, crevassed glaciers of the huge north-east face up which runs a climb graded PD for which ice axe, crampons and rope are most definitely required. At Lago Helado, a small cold-looking lake nestling under the cliffs of Cilindro, the route, hitherto north-west from the summit, turns south-west and drops quickly back to the Goriz hut. On the way back, the ledge above the waterfall was crossed with scarcely a thought, leaving me wondering why I had balked at it on the ascent. I am glad I did though, as it meant we turned the climb into a bit of a circular route, always more interesting than going up and down exactly the same way. Those wanting to do the same can either use the route described here or else that given in the Battagel guide. I have not explored that one but it involves crossing the head of the Glaciar de Ramond and then, if using this as the descent route, dropping down towards the distinctive isolated block of rocks called the Morron de Arrablo before traversing the southern slopes of Perdido to intercept the standard route.

Back at our camp after just six hours, I had some coffee and soup and then set out to explore the route to the Brèche de Roland.

Both the trail guides have rather alarming descriptions of part of this, mentioning crumbling ledges, and steel cables aiding difficult sections and we had wondered about the advisability of carrying heavy packs over such terrain. I was surprised then to arrive at the Brèche, a huge notch carved out of the cliffs of the Cirque de Gavarnie, without encountering any problems at all. A large herd of isard encountered on the path was the highlight of this, by necessity, rather fast reconnaissance. Four hours after leaving I was back in camp announcing to Alain and Mark that the way back to Gavarnie was open. That evening the most strange lenticular clouds formed, looking like giant pink flying saucers in the dying light of the already invisible sun. Such clouds usually mark high winds so I was unsurprised when at 4 a.m. I was woken by a strong gusty wind rattling the tent, a wind that was still blowing as a red and fiery dawn broke. The sky remained blue, however, though it was much colder and for the first time windproofs and hats and gloves were dragged from the depths of our packs. The still air temperature was 4°C (39°F).

From the Circo de Goriz and the white limestone cliffs of the Faja Luenga the path crosses the wide desolate spaces of the Llano y Cuello de Millaris and the Plano de San Ferlius, from whose flat basin the streams run into the Circo de Cotatuero and then the Ordesa Canyon. There are many scenic potential camp sites in this area as, despite the arid nature of the terrain, there are large patches of grass and several streams. Beyond the 2,488m (8,161ft) Collado del Descargado, cairns lead through the jumble of huge boulders into the mouth of the cirque below the Brèche de Roland. Somewhere here a path cuts north below the entrance of the Grotte Casteret, a major cave system, to the Col des Isards and the walls of the cirque. This is the route that is protected at an exposed section

by chains but it is not necessary to use it. Indeed, I never found the start of it on the Spanish side, while the easier route is fairly clear although it involves a little loss in height. Once into the bowl below the Brèche, the path heads steeply up the scree slopes on the right-hand side to pass under the walls and reach the gap itself. As we hauled our way up the scree we could see a party edging across under the walls above, clinging on to the drooping chains. They moved slowly and one at a time, and I for one was glad we were on an easier if still arduous route.

The 2,807m (9,207ft) Brèche de Roland itself is a fine spot, a perfect doorway framed by surprisingly thin soaring rock walls that reach up 100m (328ft). The gap itself is 40m (131ft) wide. The name comes from the ancient French epic poem 'The Song of Roland' which tells how Roland and the rearguard of the retreating army of Charlemagne, which was under his command, were attacked and defeated by pursuing Saracens. The dying Roland dashed his magic sword against the rock in an attempt to break it but it was the rock that split. How or when the Brèche de Roland became connected with this is unknown, the actual battle taking place at Roncevaux, 100km (62 miles) west of Gavarnie.

Reaching the Brèche is the key to the ascent of many of the summits along the rim of the cirque. The quickest and simplest to climb is the 3,144m (10,312ft) Le Taillon, a pyramid of rock and scree at the far western end of the cirque. Le Taillon vies, in fact, with Pic de Campbieil (*see* the next chapter) as the easiest 3,000m (9,840ft) peak in the Pyrenees and is worth ascending for the view alone. Heavy packs can be left at the Brèche. To begin with, the path stays close under the cliffs on the Spanish side but soon these tail off and a wider gap, known as the False Brèche, is reached. A rock pillar called, for obvious reasons, Le Doigt, is also bypassed.

Alain Kahan and Mark Edgington climbing out of the Circo de Soasco.

From here the climb becomes direct with the final stony slopes of Le Taillon lying straight ahead.

On my ascent, the cool wind had blown away any heat haze and the light was crystal clear. The views are tremendous and all-encompassing. To the north-west, the Vingemale is prominent, with its great white tumbling glacier while beyond it lies the Balaitous and waves of peaks stretching into the west. To the east, the massive Pic du Marbore-Cilindro-Monte Perdido ridge dominates the scene. Below the first lies the east wall of the Cirque de Gavarnie in all its complex glory. Standing clear to the north-east is the Neouvielle massif with more peaks out to the east. A better view into the cirque can be obtained by following Le Taillon's east ridge a short way before descending back to the Doigt and the path to the Brèche.

Back at the Brèche, Mark and I collected our packs, and Alain, who had waited there for us, passed through the gateway back into France, and set off down the steep, rough and slippery snow and scree slopes of the tiny Glacier de la Brèche (a staff is of great help in staying upright here) to the Refuge de Sarradets (also called the Refuge de la Brèche). This is, understandably, one of the most popular in the Pyrenees, given its superb situation and ease of access from the Port de Gavarnie. The hut is set on rock and there is nowhere round about really suitable for camping, though we noted one tent that had somehow been squeezed on to a flattish patch of ground right up against the walls of the refuge.

The path below the hut weaves its way down through some large boulders and then divides. The clearer more-used left-hand branch descends gently below Le Taillon to the Port de Gavarnie and is the route for those who have left their cars at the pass. Those who have walked from Gavarnie need to take the lower route, which drops steeply in a series of switchbacks beside a rushing torrent fed by the Glacier du Taillon, to reach the Vallée de Pouey Aspe a kilometre below the Cabane de Soldats and connect with the path on which we started. If you cannot quite face the immediate return to the bustle of the village, a final camp in the Pouey Aspe might appeal, though I must admit that the thought of a good meal in one of Gavarnie's restaurants had us pushing on into the town.

If you have a day to spare in Gavarnie, the ascent of Pimene, the 2,801m (9,187ft) minor peak that rises due east of the village, is well worth the 1,500m (4,920ft) ascent. I have included it here, though it could be done as an appetizer or chaser to the other routes that start or finish in Gavarnie described in the first chapter and the following chapter. The ascent starts on the southern edge of the village where a good waymarked path climbs steeply up forested slopes to the pastures of the Plateau de Pailla and the PNP Refuge des Espuguettes, below which I watched a large and noisy flock of vultures feasting on a dead sheep. From the hut, the path continues eastwards before forking. The right branch goes to the Hourquette d'Alans (*see* next chapter); the left zigzags up to Pimène's south ridge then cuts below this on the west side before returning to it for the last easy and entertaining scramble along a narrow rocky arête to the summit. Unfortunately for me, the summit itself was swathed in cloud on my only ascent so I am quoting others when I say that the view is meant to be splendid. Certainly, the vista of the Cirque de Gavarnie from the lower slopes is fine and I was granted a few impressive glimpses of walls of the Cirque d'Estaube through the clouds during the initial stages of the descent.

On the return I took the path running south below the Plateau de Pailla into the cirque, an interesting route cut into the rock walls in places and passing through some attractive woodland. It reaches the floor of the cirque at the Hotel du Cirque from where the main trail can be taken back to the village.

ROUTE

Distance		Place	Elevation	
[km]	[miles]		[metres]	[feet]
0.0	0.0	Gavarnie	1,375	4,510
5.0	3.0	Cabane de Soldats	1,954	6,409
7.0	4.5	Port de Gavarnie	2,270	7,446
12.0	7.5	San Nicolas de Bujaruelo	1,338	4,389
20.0	12.5	Puente de los Navarros	1,020	3,346
25.0	15.5	Ordesa National Park car park	1,360	4,461
32.0	20.0	Las Gradas	1,660	5,445
37.0	23.0	Refugio de Goriz	2,170	7,118
44.0	27.5	Brèche de Roland	2,804	9,197
47.0	29.0	Vallée de Pouey Aspe	1,900	6,232
51.0	31.5	Gavarnie	1,375	4,510

The ascent of Monte Perdido adds 8km (5 miles) and 1,200m (3,936ft) of ascent to this itinerary.

From Garvarnie, take the path past the church that heads towards the cirque and climbs up the west side of the valley to enter the Vallée de Pouey Aspe. Follow this past the tiny Cabane de Soldats to the Port de Gavarnie and the entry into Spain. Descend the Lapazosa valley to the bridge at San Nicolas de Bujaruelo. Do not cross the bridge but take the path (waymarked as the GR11) that runs downstream on the left bank of the Rio Ara to join the road where it crosses from the right bank. Take the road to the Puente de los Navarros. The village of Torla lies 6km (3½ miles) downstream from the bridge. If not going to Torla, turn up the road into the Ordesa Canyon and follow this to the car park, from where a path leads up the canyon past the cascades of Las Gradas to the Circo de Soasco. Then it climbs out of the canyon and traverses limestone terraces to the Refugio de Goriz, the base for the ascent of Monte Perdido which takes a day and involves a round trip of 8km (5 miles) and 1,200m (3,936ft) of ascent. From the hut, the through-route continues to climb on a clear path via the Plana de San Ferlus to the Brèche de Roland. From the Brèche, Le Taillon lies 2km (1¼ miles) and 340m (1,115ft) of ascent to the west. From the Brèche, descend steeply back into France and past the Refuge des Sarradets, and on back down into the Vallée de Pouey Aspe and from there Gavarnie.

MAPS

IGN Carte de Randonnees 1:50,000 No. 4 Bigorre. Editorial Alpina 1:40,000 Valle de Ordesa.

TRAIL GUIDES

Battagel, Arthur, *Pyrenees West* (Gaston West Col)
Reynolds, Kev, *Walks and Climbs in the Pyrenees* (Cicerone Press)

A Traverse of the Neouvielle Massif:

Barèges to Gavarnie with an ascent of the Pic de Campbieil

> *There is a pleasure in camping on mountains inexplicable to the unbeliever, but which will be at once apparent to anyone of imagination.*
>
> **W.H. Murray**

Giant bright 'butterflies' floating down from the deep blue skies greeted the three of us as we headed out of the little French village of Barèges. Spiralling down towards the green meadows below they were soon revealed as parapentes (wing-shaped parachutes used in paragliding). Their take-off point was high above us on the slopes of the Pic d'Ourdegouns. Watching them took the sting out of the first climb which was steep, though also thankfully tree-shaded. It was hard for us to believe as we sweated up the path that just over twenty-four hours before we had left behind the grim, grey dullness of an English September.

Our plan, tentative and open to change at any time, was to link the Neouvielle massif, a huge block of granite mountains lying wholly in France and well north of the main chain of the Pyrenees, with the great cirques of Barroude, Troumouse and Estaube on the frontier to the south. *En route* we intended to climb a few peaks and explore some remote valleys. We had food and fuel for a week or more and no desire to hurry. The element of doubt and route-finding interest in the plan was that the maps showed no paths between the Neouvielle and the ranges to the south. We had a couple of ideas for ways across the

mountains that barred our way but no real idea if these were feasible. The route we put together, incorporating sections of the GR10 and the HRP plus less well-known paths and some cross-country sections, is the one described here. Unlike most of those in this book it is neither a circular nor a linear route but a meandering one, linking several very different areas.

The route starts in Barèges, a popular tourist village offering all facilities, including bus services. It lies to the north of the Neouvielle and on the road to the Col du Tourmalet, a famous name to cyclists as it is a major climb on the Tour de France. There are three staffed huts on or near the route plus several basic shelters but it is not really feasible to do the walk without a tent. As there are a myriad high-level mountain sites to choose from, it would be wasting the walk's potential not to take one. Most of the route lies in the Neouvielle Nature Reserve and the Pyrenees National Park which means there are restrictions on camping, however. Indeed, in the reserve it is not allowed at all except at two rather overused and unattractive roadside sites. However, it is possible to arrange the itinerary for the walk so as to pass through the heart of the reserve without the need for

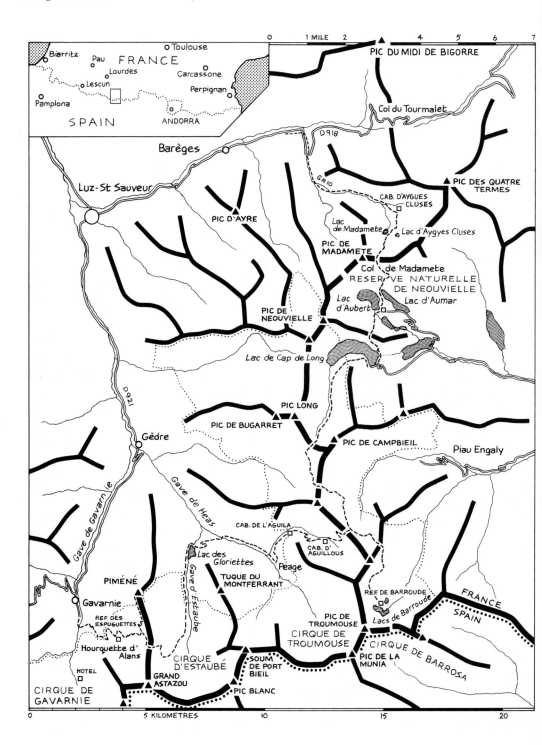

an overnight stop. In the PNP the rule applies about camping only an hour or more's walk from the nearest road.

Although the distance is short (60km/38 miles), there is much ascent and some difficult terrain to cross plus a great variety of scenery to observe as well as some recommended side trips, so I would suggest allowing at least five days and preferably a week or more for the trek. Most of the walking is on waymarked and clear trails but the central cross-country section involves the crossing of a high ridge and then the careful picking out of a safe route across a steep and rocky mountainside. As this section is unavoidable, this is not really a walk for those unused to or unhappy with off-trail travel.

Initially, though, you have the red paint splashes and wide trail of the GR10 to follow. This parallels the road for several kilometres from Barèges before leaving it to begin a long, slow haul up the Coubous valley. Alain Kahan, Mark Edgington and I undertook this climb in the heat of the afternoon, having arrived in Barèges late morning. Above, the sun beat painfully down. To either side great grey scree slopes spread over the hillsides above the flower-filled meadows and the gradually dwindling conifer forest. Marmots called from the boulder fields as we passed, while kestrels hung in the bright blue sky. Mark reacted to the ever more impressive scenery with the excitement and amazement of one who had never been backpacking outside Britain before. Alain and I, veterans of several previous Pyrenean ventures, were more blasé. It will get much better, we said. Secretly, though, I envied Mark the pleasure of a first encounter with the Pyrenees.

About 3km (1¾ miles) up the valley, a trail junction is reached. We stayed on the GR10 but the right fork would make a good alternative, climbing past the Lac des Coubous to the Hourquette d'Aubert and then down to join the route described here at the Lac d'Aubert. The difference in distance between the two routes is minimal, both being about 8km (5 miles) from the junction to the lake. Soon after we had turned up the left fork into the narrower valley of the Aygues-Cluses, we crossed a small but pretty meadow fringed by a stream and a few stands of small pines. The soft turf looked inviting and the surroundings delectable so, although we had only been walking for four hours and had progressed only a little over 9km (5½ miles), we decided to stop and make camp, this spot being just too idyllic to pass by. If you do manage to pass by, however, there are others as pleasant not far ahead. We were happy to sit by the trickling stream, our stoves set up on the grass, and gaze at the splendid scenery. As dusk fell, a faint squeaking filled the air as the dark shapes of tiny bats swooped around the site. A huge bright full moon lit the clear night sky, reflecting off the pale rocks, and Mark, enthralled by this first Pyrenean camp, slept outside in his pile sleeping bag under the stars. Alain and I, not wanting to risk our down-filled bags becoming damp from any dew or a change in the weather, retreated into the tents. We need not have worried as the temperature only fell to 8°C (46°F) and there was no dew.

Another hot day ensued as we continued along the GR10 through a series of stepped meadows to the small and basic Cabane d'Aygues-Cluses which stands above a small tarn. Here the trail splits into three and again we stayed with the GR10, which this time meant taking the right branch (the left leads to the Hourquette Nère, the central one to the Col de Barège, both alternative though longer ways into the heart of the Neouvielle by way of the Lac d l'Oule and the Lac d'Oredon). The GR10 path ascends through more open, rocky terrain, with the views opening out of the rugged ridges ahead and to either side, past the pretty Lacs de Madamète to enter the Neouvielle Nature Reserve at the 2,509m (8,230ft) Col de Madamete, our first high pass. Looking down we could see the deep blue waters of the Lacs d'Aubert and d'Aumar and beyond them the highest Neouvielle peak, 3,192m (10,470ft) Pic Long, at whose foot we intended camping as it was outside the reserve. First, though, we had to descend to the lakes and then cross a high intervening ridge.

The descent was easy to Lac d'Aumar and Lac d'Aubert where there is a roadhead and a rough, overused campsite. If you are feeling at all weary this is the place to stop for the day, though, as there is still a long way to go before there is anywhere else you can camp. Those seeking a little more luxury can follow the road 6km (3¾ miles) to the Chalet-Hotel d'Oredon. The route, however, leaves the GR10 which heads off to the east and crosses the Aubert dam to start an ascent on an orange/white/orange paint-blazed path. This soon fades away to leave a steep climb up rough and finally rocky slopes to the 2,465m (8,085ft) Pas de Gat on the crest of the ridge above. From here there is an impressive view straight down to the large deep blue curve of the Lac de Cap de Long, which seems to lie directly below your feet. It feels like that throughout the descent, too, which is on a very steep, badly eroded and unpleasant path which requires care in places as it cuts across loose slopes and the heads of deep gullies (do not be tempted to try to descend these as there are cliffs below) towards the dam at the east end of the lake.

There is no water on this tedious and

The Barroude Wall.

lengthy section so it is advisable to fill water bottles at the Lac d'Aubert. We had neglected to do this so the cafés at the roadhead, a popular tourist destination, at the far side of the dam were welcome, especially as the day was very hot and we had now been out for a long while. Cokes, coffees, pizzas, salads and an hour's rest set us up for the final kilometres on a good path across steep slopes above the southern shore of the Lac de Cap de Long to a good pitch at the far end by a small stream outside the Nature Reserve. We were now in the Pyrenees National Park, as is most of the rest of the walk. Across the lake, the slopes we had descended looked precipitous. We had walked 19km (11¾ miles) but it had taken ten hours. A camp higher up the Aygues-Cluses valley or even by the Lacs de Madamète would shorten the day a little.

During the evening, rain began to fall and a wind rattled the tents. Dawn came with mist over the peaks and squally showers. Ahead of us lay the problematic part of the route. I hoped that we could find a route down the far side of the pass known as the Hourquette de Cap de Long that lay directly south of our camp on the ridge between Pic Long and 3,173m (10,407ft) Pic de Campbieil. If we could descend into the Campbieil valley below from the pass then we could pick up marked paths again. An initial exploration seemed in order before hauling full loads the 800m (2,624ft) to the pass in case the prospective route proved impossible and we had to rethink our plans, so Mark and I set off with just one light pack between us to reconnoitre the route. The climb is fairly straightforward as you cannot really go wrong in ascending a valley like this, though there are a few rockbands to be climbed or bypassed as you choose. There are vague traces of a path plus a few cairns but mostly you make your own way past a series of attractive waterfalls from lush meadows into ever more rocky terrain. The

climb levels out into a cirque immediately below the pass; here we found some fascinating rock scenery including some shallow caves where bands of limestones cut through the granite. Round the grey waters of the Gourg de Cap de Long lay a sterile, arid world of stone; cold and unfriendly in the dull, soft light. Cairns lead over the rubble to the 2,902m (9,519ft) pass. From here a short descent down the scree to the south revealed what seemed to be a steep and pathless but feasible way into the valley below.

With the next day's route roughly worked out, we turned our attention to Pic de Campbieil, ascending by an easy scramble along its south-west ridge. Alpine choughs flitted in and out of the mist around us as did the views from the small, neat but cold and windswept summit. In clear conditions I imagine the vista is magnificent. A switch-backing path leads back down the steep loose scree of the mountain's western flanks to the Gourg de Cap de Long. It makes for a fast descent but I would not like to climb it. Pic Long can also be ascended from the west end of Lac de Cap de Long, though this is more of a real climb, with the guidebooks recommending rope and crampons. We did not have these but we would have at least 'gone to have a look' if the weather had been better. As it was, we contented ourselves with the glimpses of the peak and its attendant small glaciers granted us through the clouds. Rain started to fall again as we reached camp but faded enough for us to sit round a small fire lit with wood scavenged from the shores of the lake. During the night, however, the downpour grew heavier.

Though the thick low cloud completely covering the sky at dawn was not promising, a few patches of blue gave us hope the next morning as we began the climb again, fully loaded this time, in dense, swirling wet mist. Behind us an even thicker blanket of grey rolled in along the lake, smothering the view. Surprisingly and luckily, it was clear at the pass so we could see our planned route as we began the descent, cutting southwards across the slopes to try to hit the path up the Campbieil valley to the 2,596m (8,515ft) Port de Campbieil as high as possible. Care is needed on this descent as there are loose shaly bluffs and ledges interspersed with steep scree to scramble down before a grassy terrace is reached. Here we re-entered thick wet mist. Our navigation by sight abruptly curtailed, we continued across steep loose scree slopes on a compass bearing (south), spread out but careful not to lose sight of one another. Rumbles of thunder suggested worsening weather as we suddenly stumbled on the clear zigzags of the next path, but thankfully the worst of the storm passed us by, though a burst of heavy rain had us donning full waterproofs before we reached the top of the pass.

The steep switchbacking descent east from

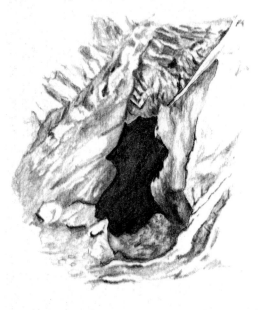

Limestone cave near the Port de Campbieil.

the Port de Campbieil leads to a junction where the right fork is taken to begin a long southerly traverse above the upper Badet valley. This intersects the Haute Route Pyrénée below the Hourquette de Heas. We did this in nil visibility. Crossing another pass did not appeal after a long day in bad weather, so we headed east hoping to find a camp site at the head of the Badet valley. Pitches for the tents were located quickly amongst the grassy hummocks but the area seemed dry (the map shows intermittent streams), so we adopted my usual strategy in such circumstances which is to drop the packs and search for water, canteens in hand. Downhill is usually the best direction to go in, and so it proved for we soon located a line of cairns leading down a gully in which, just before it steepened too much, we found a trickle of water. We were very grateful for this as the day had been hard and we were quite tired, and the descent into the valley bottom where water was guaranteed looked steep and difficult. In fact, unless you are willing to lose a great deal of height, this is the only good site between Lac de Cap de Long and the Aguillous valley on the far side of the Heas pass. Therefore, although it is off the through-route, I recommend using it, especially as it makes a good base for a quick visit to the Barroude Wall.

We had camped with no idea of our surroundings so it was with delight and surprise that we looked out the next morning on to a superb sunlit view with the peaks of the Neouvielle spread out to the north beyond the curving line of the Badet valley, a vista spectacular enough to take our minds off the rather chilly 3°C (37°F) temperature. Being close to the Barroude Wall, Mark and I decided to take a look at this famed limestone precipice so, leaving Alain contemplating a prolonged breakfast and a snooze in the sun, we set off over the Hourquette de Chermentas and along a fine contouring path. This led under the great overhanging walls of the Pic de la Gela, which had Mark, a rock climber, gazing upwards with interest and awe and trying out a few low moves, into the heart of the cirque where lie the Lacs de Barroude and also a small staffed PNP refuge.

The cliff scenery here is magnificent with the unbroken main wall that runs for 2km (1¼ miles) north–south from the Pic de Gerbats to the Pic de Troumouse, and which in fact makes up the eastern edge of the Cirque de Troumouse, visible in all its glory as it rises 400–500m (1,312–1,640ft) from the scree below. There are, not surprisingly, many difficult rock climbs on these cliffs. To the south lies the wide 2,534m (8,312ft) Pas de Barroude over which a path leads into Spain and the Circo del Barrosa. Like all paths in the Pyrenees, it tempts the walker on to go

and see what lies beyond. With reluctance, we turned our eyes away and retraced our steps, our route lying in the other direction.

Back in camp, we spread out our damp gear to dry in the now hot sun before turning west for the steep, though short climb that ends suddenly at 2,608m (8,554ft) Hourquette de Heas, a deep notch in a thin, rocky arête, reached from both sides over slabs and narrow ledges. This pass is a superb viewpoint and we gazed for some time at the vista in front of us which was dominated by the vast mass of the Vingemale, its rock buttresses split by the pale spread of the Glacier d'Ossoue, and the crest of the Cirque de Gavarnie with the deep cleft of the Brèche de Roland the prominent feature.

Much closer lay the impressive long summit ridge of the 2,976m (9,761ft) Soum des Sallettes, beneath which we descended on a

Descent from the Plateau de Cardous into the Gavarnie valley.

The view north from the Hourquette de Chermentas.

good path to the grassy flats of the Montagne des Aiguillous, where there is a small shepherd's hut (the Cabane des Aiguillous). From here, the path meanders on down into a pleasant limestone bowl complete with dry streambeds, green pastures and other features typically found in such terrain. This bowl leads to another, this time with a stream, in which we camped right on the national park boundary near the Cabane de l'Aguila, a basic refuge, and the small wild-flower-decorated shrine of the Fontaine et Oratoire de la Ste-Famille, carved out of soapstone and with a spring seeping out of its base.

A short brush with civilization began the next day as we descended steeply to the tiny hamlet of Heas, passing *en route* a trail crew at work, with mini-bulldozer and dynamite, on rebuilding the HRP. To the south of Heas lies the huge Cirque de Troumouse, the largest in the range and 4km (2½ miles) in diameter. An 8–10km (5–6 mile) round trip from Heas provides a closer view of this massive natural amphitheatre. The highest point on its almost level top is 3,133m (10,276ft) Pic de La Munia whose ascent involves a PD grade climb and the use of rope and crampons. The walk to the cirque can be done on the road that climbs up the west side of the valley or, preferably, by the trail in the valley bottom.

The through-route turns away from the cirque at Heas and follows the road west for a few kilometres to the Lac des Gloriettes dam and the last part of the walk. There are cafés and camp grounds along the road. An easy and pleasant wander in meadows ensues up the Estaube valley from the lake (many potential campsites here). There are excellent views ahead to the headwall of the Cirque de Estaube which harbours two passes into Spain, the difficult Brèche de Tuquerouye (ice axes, crampons and rope required), first climbed by Ramond de Carbonierres in 1797 during an attempt on Monte Perdido which lies directly

to the south, and the easier Port de Pinède which leads into the Valle de Pineta.

As the head of the cirque is approached, the route turns gradually into an increasingly steep climb up the west side of the valley. Where the path divides, take the right-hand branch (the left leads to the two passes) which leads to the 2,430m (7,970ft) Hourquette d'Alans, another narrow notch of a pass that gives excellent views of the 3,071m (10,073ft) Grand Astazou immediately to the south and the rest of the Cirque de Gavarnie. From the pass, the path drops down to the undulating grasslands of the Plateau de Cardous where we set up camp by a small stream. For the first time another tent was pitched in the same area, while just over a small ridge lay the wardened Refuge des Espuguettes. This is a superb spot. To the east rises the ridge from which we had descended running from Pimène (which can be climbed easily from the description in the previous chapter), in the north the Grand Astazou. The latter marks the start of the curve of walls of the Cirque de Gavarnie which can be followed round over the gash of the Brèche de Roland to the pyramid of Le Taillon. Beyond that peak, the horizon drops away to the low point of the Pont de Gavarnie and then, dominating the view further round to the north, the Vingemale rises above a welter of lesser summits.

The final dawn of the walk came softly in pastel shades of pink on the peaks across the valley, the light making the scene look more like a painting than reality. Then suddenly swathes of clouds swept in and the valley turned white and the peaks vanished. We packed up and walked down the trail through the meadows with excellent views of the walls of the cirque appearing and disappearing in the clouds. The path then dropped into the cool of the forest to emerge in the valley and cross the Gave de Gavarnie by the stone Pont de Nadau on to the road 2km (1¼ miles) south of Gavarnie and into the noise of tourists and horses and cafés and cars. We did not mind. After a day here we would be ready to go on again, over into Spain on another Pyrenean adventure.

ROUTE

Distance		Place	Elevation	
[km]	[miles]		[metres]	[feet]
0.0	0.0	Barèges	1,240	4,067
5.0	3.0	Pont de la Gaubie	1,538	5,045
11.0	7.0	Cabane d'Aygues-Cluses	2,150	7,052
14.0	8.5	Col de Madamète	2,509	8,230
17.0	10.5	Lac d'Aubert	2,150	7,052
19.0	12.0	Pas du Gat	2,465	8,085
20.0	12.5	Lac de Cap de Long dam	2,160	7,085
28.0	17.5	Hourquette de Cap de Long	2,902	9,519
31.0	19.5	Port de Campbieil	2,596	8,515
35.0	22.0	Hourquette de Heas	2,608	8,554
39.0	24.0	Fontaine et Oratoire de la Ste-Famille	1,900	6,232
42.0	26.0	Chapelle de Heas	1,521	4,988
46.0	28.5	Lac des Gloriettes	1,668	5,471
54.0	33.5	Hourquette d'Alans	2,430	7,970
56.0	35.0	Refuge des Espugeuttes	2,043	6,701
61.0	38.0	Gavarnie	1,375	4,510

The above is the basic route and does not include the ascent of Pic de Campbieil or the side trips to the Barroude Wall and the Troumouse and Estaube Cirques.

The walk starts in Barèges and initially heads east on the clearly marked GR10, paralleling the road leading to the Col du Tourmalet but leaving this at the Pont de la Gaubie, after having turned south to ascend the Coubous valley. At the first trail junction stay on the GR10, now heading south-east up the Aygues-Cluses valley to the small Cabane d'Aygues-Cluses. Here it turns south-westwards and climbs into more open country to pass the Lacs de Madamète and reach the Col de Madamète where the Neouvielle Nature Reserve is entered. Descend from the col past the little Gourg de Rabas tarn to the Lac d'Aumar where the GR10 is left and a linking path taken to the nearby Lac d'Aubert where there is a roadhead camp site.

The route now crosses the dam and then ascends steeply on a paint-blazed but intermittent path to the Pas du Gat on the ridge above. From here a narrow, badly eroded path cuts south-east across the very steep mountainside to the Lac de Cap de Long dam. This is crossed to the cafés at the far side, from where a track leads along and then above the south shore of the reservoir to its west end. Less clear paths now lead up the valley to the south to the Hourquette de Cap de Long, from where Pic de Campbieil (3,173m) can easily be climbed and where the cross-country section starts. Begin this by descending the scree slightly to the south-west of the pass to avoid some small crags directly below, but very soon turn south and angle across the steep scree, rock and grass to intercept the switchbacks of the path leading up the valley below and follow these to the Port de Campbieil. Descend steeply eastwards from the pass on a good path to a trail junction. Here take the path climbing to the south and follow this over grassy terraces and rocky slopes to another trail junction where the Haute Route Pyrénée is joined.

The through-route is by the right-hand branch here but those who wish to see the Barroude Wall should first take the left-hand one up past a good camping area to the Hourquette de Chermentas and then into the Barroude cirque, a round trip from the trail junction of 10–12km (6–7½ miles), depending on how far into the cirque you go. Back at the trail junction, the right fork leads up to the Hourquette de Heas and then down into the pastures of the Aguillous valley past the Fontaine et Oratoire de la Ste-Famille and further down to the road below at the Chapelle de Heas. The road is now followed westwards (turn left at the junction) to the dammed Lac des Gloriettes, from where a path leads south along the west shore of the lake and then up the Estaube valley. Near the head of the valley, the path switchbacks up the west wall to the Hourquette d'Alans, from where it descends to the Plateau de Cardous and then past the Refuge des Espugeuttes, into the forest and down to Gavarnie.

MAPS

IGN Carte de Randonnées 1:50,000 No. 4 Bigorre. IGN Serie Bleue 1:25,000 1747 ouest Luz-St-Sauveur, 1748 ouest Gavarnie.

TRAIL GUIDE

No guide details all this route but Kev Reynolds' *Walks and Climbs in the Pyrenees* (Cicerone Press) covers most of it.

A Tour of Luchon:

Port d'Oo, Port de Venasque, Pico de Posets, Pico de Aneto and Pic de Maupas

> It was crackling cold. The stream across the slope had been silenced by frost and my breath had rimed my sleeping bag with white hoar. It was completely quiet. I found myself holding my breath and straining my ears for a noise, any noise. Surely the stars should sing!
>
> **Hamish Brown**
> **The Great Walking Adventure**

Although not quite as conveniently placed as Gavarnie, Bagnères-de-Luchon (Luchon for short) is another of those places that every walker in the Pyrenees eventually visits. For me it was the first place in the range I ever visited, alighting there from the Paris train with Alain Kahan and Graham Huntington for my first walk in the region. Unlike Gavarnie, Luchon is a rather stylish, fashionable town with wide boulevards, expensive boutiques and pavement cafés. Wandering through it with a large pack, one feels more than a little out of place yet it is the starting point for many possible mountain adventures. As well as the convenience of rail access, it does boast some basic campsites and reasonably cheap cafés so you are not forced to stay in a swish hotel. There are mountaineering stores in the town, too, so any items you may have forgotten can be purchased here, as can maps and guides in one of the several bookshops. It is also a good place to have breakfast after the overnight train journey from Paris before you head off into the mountains.

Immediately south of Luchon, deep forested valleys lead up to high peaks and the central and highest part of the longest continuous section of the frontier which stretches, un-broken by any road crossing (though there are two tunnels carrying highways beneath the mountains), from the Col de Portalet by the Pic du Midi d'Ossau and the Bonaigue pass east of the Encantados. Eight summits are over 3,000m (9,840ft) high and there are several major passes for the adventurous walker to explore. If this is not enough, beyond the frontier in Spain there lie the two highest summits in the range, 3,375m (11,070ft) Pico de Posets and 3,404m (11,165ft) Pico de Aneto, their massifs divided by the valley of the Rio Esera. The walk described here offers ascents of both these mountains and crosses the frontier by two high passes. It wanders through some of the French valleys and provides an opportunity to climb a number of other peaks. The route will take most people about a week to complete without any of the ascents. With them, plus perhaps a day or two off from walking, a fortnight is not too long. However, it is possible to shorten the route by using a car or taxi to start or finish (or both) at a roadhead some way out of Luchon. In total, doing so cuts out 24km (15 miles) of walking and a great deal of ascent.

Although, as always, I recommend camping, enough staffed refuges and basic shelters lie on or near the route for it to be done

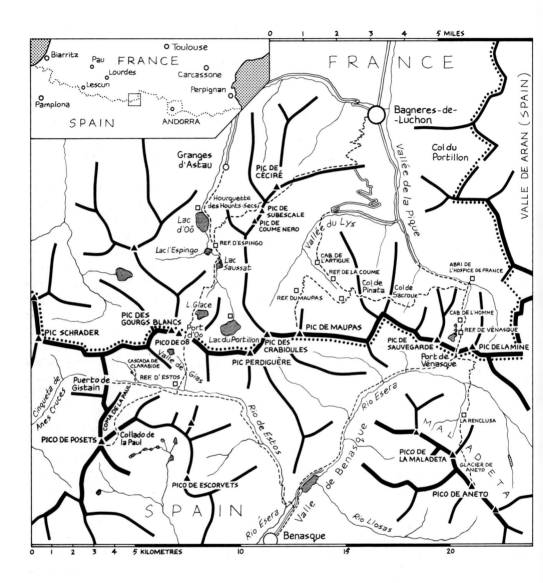

without the need for camping gear, but doing so would involve some long days. However, those intent on climbing peaks that require mountaineering gear may well want to stay in huts in order to cut down on the weight carried. Otherwise, there are many fine sites for the camper to use.

The full route starts by following the GR10 south out of Luchon up the steep switchbacks of an old bobsleigh run to the hill overlooking the town. On this stands the Hôtel de Super-bagnères (shops, hotels, bars and, possibly, a bus from Luchon if you want to avoid the initial climb). The path bypasses this to traverse below the 2,403m (7,882ft) Pic de Cécire and to cross the 2,275m (7,462ft) Hourquette des Hounts-Secs before descending to the staffed CAF Refuge d'Espingo.

Here, the shorter alternative start to the walk comes in from the north. This starts at the Granges d'Astau to which a taxi can be caught from Luchon (there is no bus and if you leave a car here you will have to come back and collect it, so a taxi makes most sense). The clear path, again a section of the GR10, ascends from the Astau valley by a series of switchbacks to the Lac d'Oo, the climb enhanced by the myriad flowers that bloom alongside it. The lake is a popular tourist destination and has a café on its southern shore, a welcome source of refreshment on a hot day. It is a beautiful spot with rugged mountainsides dropping down to the lake and a fine thin waterfall curving down into the water. The path skirts the east shore for a short way and then climbs up to the Espingo hut.

The two starts now combined, the route continues as the HRP up to Lac Saussat where there are many good, if overused, sites. I have particularly fond memories of camping here as it was my first overnight stop in the Pyrenees and I had never been in such high mountains before. Dawn came with a haze and high clouds but the summits were clear as we set off up the superb stone slab path of the HRP. This is left in the shallow Coume de l'Abesque for cairns that lead over boulders and rough slopes under the rust- and grey-banded crags of the north face of 3,065m (10,053ft) Pic des Spijoles (which can be easily climbed from here – see details in *Pyrenees East* by Arthur Battagel). It overlooks the dark blue, ice-floe-covered Lac Glace set in a deep, steep-sided cirque ringed by peaks, glaciers and snowfields – this is truly a magnificent spot.

From here on to the pass there may be several snow patches, some extensive, to be negotiated even late in the season. We crossed a small one above the lake before following cairns along a series of ledges to the south.

Next comes another, larger and permanent snowfield, the Seil de la Baque glacier, that runs up to the Col des Gourgs Blancs to the west. The angle being gentle and the snow firm, we stayed on it for as long as possible before undertaking the final climb up boulders and loose scree to the 2,908m (9,538ft) Port d'Oo and a first view into Spain. Despite a cold wind that had us changing from shorts to breeches, we sat on the ridge for half an hour marvelling at the wild vista spread out before us with the Pico de Posets, although hazy, dominant across the Valle de Estos.

The route into that valley is not as obvious as it looks on the Editorial Alpina map whose contour lines suggest a smooth, uniform slope. The reality is totally different: a steep, rugged mountainside of small crags, boulder fields and scree lying below the pass. This makes the descent quite difficult, especially as the map is no help at all, though there are cairns in places marking the way. The route swings back and forth across the slopes but always well to the east of the Lagos de Gias which can be seen to the right. Eventually, the stream running out of these lakes is crossed and a path picked up that leads down into stands of black pine and to the FEM Refugio de Estos, a large new hut standing on a bluff above the river (or so I am told – the old hut burnt down in 1979 and I have not seen the new one with my own eyes). Those who wish to camp, as we did, will find several good sites upstream from the hut, though those close to it have been rather overused. We pitched our tents quite a way west of the hut on a grassy patch on the right bank of the river with excellent views up the valley. The rich greenness of the valley bottom here is a great contrast to the grey aridity of the slopes above.

There is so much interesting country to explore in the Estos region that it is worth staying here for a few days even if you are not planning on an ascent of Pico de Posets, the

Graham Huntington on the Port d'Oo.

obvious day trip from the valley. For the botanist, the Estos valley is a paradise, and Alain had spent his time searching out rarities around our campsite the day after our arrival. Meanwhile, Graham and I headed west up the valley to climb the final rough slopes to the Puerto de Gistain, a 2,592m (8,502ft) pass on the ridge, linking the Posets massif with the frontier ridge that provides excellent views into the upper Cinqueta valley (the staffed Refugio de Viados lies further down this vale) and across to the peaks on the far side. From the pass it is worth scrambling up to the minor peak (spot height 2,790m/9,151ft) that lies at the end of a narrow, rocky ridge directly to the north. From here there are wider views east covering the long Estos valley and beyond it the distant Maladetta, with to the south the high and imposing bulk of Pico de Posets and to the north the frontier peaks running west to the bulk of 3,174m (10,411ft) Grande Bachimala (also known as Pic Schrader). Before the Puerto de Gistain is reached, the Clarabide stream enters the Estos from the north, rushing out of a narrow steep-walled gorge. This short ravine is worth venturing into as it ends where the Cascada de Clarabide tumbles down a high cliff, a dramatic waterfall unseen from outside.

As well as a list of flowers, Alain had also collected some fallen wood from the edges of the stream to which we added the sadly large amount of litter we found on this and nearby camp sites before piling the lot into a well-used fire ring and burning it. It was pleasant to sit round the fire as darkness fell, though a heavy shower had us scurrying back into the tents at one point. A few rumbles of thunder showed that more rain was around.

Our plans for the next day had been for an ascent of Pico de Posets. These plans were thrown into doubt at 12.45 a.m. when we were woken by a thunderstorm breaking overhead and torrential rain lashing the tents. This first burst of storm lasted an hour or so and then deteriorated into steady drizzle and low cloud. Our climb cancelled, we spent a lazy morning brewing up and reading in the tents. This peaceful interlude was shattered in the early afternoon by the arrival of an even more violent electric storm accompanied by even heavier rain that soon threatened to swamp the site. Alain's small solo tent was pitched on a raised bit of ground, quite safe from any flood danger. The larger dome tent Graham and I were using was, however, pitched on the lowest, flattest area and we soon had water running under the groundsheet. Reluctantly we slipped out into the downpour, bare-legged and bare-footed but with water-proof jackets on, to dig shallow drainage trenches with our ice axes. In principle, I am against doing this but faced with being washed off the site, I found my principles suddenly vanishing. After the storm was over we did try to replace the earth we had removed and return the site as far as possible to how we had found it, which was, anyway, bare of vegetation and hard packed due to repeated use. This in itself was one reason for the pitch flooding.

Thankfully, the storm fully cleared over-night so Graham and I set out early the next morning intent on climbing the Pico de Posets. A rough path leads up and across the hillside away from the river to pass under the impressive convoluted rock faces of the Aguja de la Paul and the Tuca de la Paul and curve into the Coma de la Paul. Rather than the snow mentioned in the trail guides, we found the route in this valley to be mostly over loose boulders and scree all the way to the Collado de la Paul at its head. Pico de Posets, the

secondest highest peak in the Pyrenees, was first climbed in 1856. By the *voie normale* it is an easy peak, climbed thousands of times every year. We, however, failed. Writing this at a distance of nine years I can no longer say for certain why this was so. The fact that it was the first peak outside Britain that either of us had attempted may have had something to do with it.

What we did is clear from the notes I made afterwards. Beyond the Collado de la Paul lies another col, not marked on the map, which we assumed was the one we had to cross. Once over this, we found a gully we took to be that mentioned in the trail guides, though Graham was more doubtful than I and remained below while I scrambled up the desperately loose rock only to find large, steep slabs barring the way. After climbing carefully back down, I found that Graham had seen a climber descending the correct gully which, in fact, lies across the small glacier between the two cols. We thought of making the climb now we knew the way but massing clouds above the peak reminded us of the previous day's storm and we decided it was better to descend than risk being caught high up in a thunderstorm. To console us for our failure we had superb views of the Maladetta and the frontier peaks from the cols and also the sight of our first isards, ten of them grazing in the Coma de la Paul. Our decision to retreat was proved correct, too. We beat the rain to the tents by all of a minute.

After three days in the Estos valley (one more than we had intended because of the storm) we decided to move on, in part because we needed to pick up some supplies but also because, lovely though the Vallée de Estos is, we wanted to see more of what the Pyrenees had to offer. The nearest place in which to pick up supplies is the ancient village of Benasque in the Esera valley. This is reached by the good path that leads down beside the rushing Estos stream through groves of trees and gentle pastureland walled by the mountains that rise up on either side. This is a lovely walk, ending eventually where a road crosses the river. Three kilometres (1¾ miles) down this road lies Benasque with its stores and hotels. Just before the road, camping is possible in the fields by the river and this is where we pitched, walking into town for a restaurant meal and to buy food. Benasque has old steep-sided narrow cobbled streets whose dark, damp confines conjure up times long past but it also parades some modern concrete and steel high-rise blocks that signify the late twentieth century.

More development forces the walker to tread tarmac for too long on the ascent of the Esera valley, the link between the Posets and Maladetta massifs. The long, curving valley is beautiful but the road, meant to link with France eventually via a tunnel, is a scar that detracts badly from the surrounding splendour. It now runs all the way to the flat grasslands of the Plan d'Estany, a popular, overused and dirty camping spot where there is (or at least was in 1986) a shack serving hot drinks and snacks. From here, a wide eroded path winds upwards to the Refugio de la Renclusa, a popular and large (75 places) staffed hut that is the base for the ascent of Pico de Aneto, highest in the Pyrenees. We went on a few hundred metres past the hut to camp by a stream. If I have to camp near a hut I always prefer to do so above rather than below it in order to be sure of clean water.

The reason for camping near La Renclusa was that we, like those staying in the hut, wished to climb Aneto and follow in the foot-

Crossing the Aneto Glacier.

View from the Puerto de Gistain.

steps of the Russian officer Platon de Tchihat-cheff and the three others who made the first and second ascents in 1842. By the *voie normale* it is a relatively easy climb (Alpine grade PD) but it does involve crossing the cre-vassed Aneto Glacier so crampons, ice axe and rope should be carried. The final scramble up the large granite boulders of the Puente de Mahoma is quite exposed though not difficult. From the Renclusa hut, the well-used route climbs steeply to the narrow Cresta de los Portillones, a major watershed as streams to the west run, via the Ebro, into the Mediter-ranean, while those to the east eventually end up, via the Garonne, in the Atlantic. The rocky ridge is reached at the Portillon Inferior and is then followed south-west to the Portillon Superior from where the path descends to cross stony slopes to the glacier. I first climbed Aneto alone as the cold wind and low clouds kept Graham in camp (Alain never climbs mountains if he can avoid it) and by the time I reached the edge of the glacier I had met many people turning back. It was cold enough for me to wear pile jacket, Gore-tex jacket, balaclava and gloves.

Never having been on a glacier before, I started off very gingerly but soon found that this late in the season (it was mid-September) all the snow had gone and the crevasses were open. To avoid them, I followed the base of the Cresta to the bergschrund and then the edge of the latter to the Collado de Coronas where the direct route across the glacier is met. The snow cone above is then climbed to its top (packs can be left here) which lies below the airy but easy Puente de Mahoma rock ridge along which you scramble to the small summit. This is decorated with a large cross and various religious icons plus, when I was there, an appalling amount of litter. By the time I reached the top the clouds had mostly sunk into the French valleys to the north, leaving just the summits poking through. For thirty minutes I was alone on the roof of the Pyrenees admiring the extensive

Graham Huntington climbing out of the Cirque de la Glère.

but not really spectacular view, the feeling being one of space as everything in view is far away and lower than you are. Another party arrived just as I began the descent back to the glacier over which I returned via the direct route, stepping over the many crevasses in the wake of a party of six Spanish climbers who plied me with food and drink when we reached the other side.

The next day dawned sunny and windless and when Graham evinced an interest in climbing Aneto, I said I would go with him, so much had I enjoyed the ascent the day before. This time we crossed the centre of the glacier roped together and returned by the route along the bergschrund. Amazingly, there was hardly anybody else about. On returning to camp we found that Alain had been foraging for wood, so that evening we had a fire and also a bottle of wine he had procured from the hut. A full moon rose, the rocks reflecting its pale light and I slept out under it, spurning the protection of the tent. The dawn was chilly but dry and I lay on my back in my sleeping bag as the bright moon faded and the sun lit up the circle of summits above me and then crept down the hillside towards our camp.

There are other climbs that can be made from the Renclusa area: the Maladetta has fourteen 3,000m (9,840ft) summits apart from Aneto, many of which, including Pico de la Maladetta itself, can be ascended by easy routes from the Renclusa area, as can be some lower peaks on the frontier ridge and in the Mulleres group to the east. Many explorations can be made but the through-route heads north back into France, which is what we did after our two days in these magnificent 'accursed mountains'. After descending back to the Esera valley, the route ascends an excellent set of switchbacks to the 2,444m (8,016ft) Port de Venasque, an impressive narrow notch in the rock wall of the frontier

giving superb views of the Posets, Maladetta and, to the east, the Mullères hills. An even better viewpoint, though, is the 2,738m (8,981ft) summit of the Pic de Sauvegarde which can easily be climbed in under an hour from the pass. From the notch, you descend down very steep scree by tight switchbacks to the Refuge de Venasque, a one-roomed unstaffed CAF hut where we stayed. The situation is superb with a fine tarn next to the hut and the rock walls of the Pic de la Mine towering above, while to the north the hills fade slowly into the haze of the lowlands.

From the refuge, a good path leads down through a narrow valley into the woods below and the Pont de Penjat. If you are in a hurry to return to Luchon, as Alain was because of an appointment back home, keep straight on here to the Hospice de France and a road walk into the town. Our route, though, turns westwards at the bridge and runs through the steep beech, pine and spruce forests of the Bois de Sajust and the Bois de Bedourède on a good path, before crossing the open Cirque de la Glère and climbing steep grassy slopes to 2,034m (6,672ft) Col de Sacroux and a view again of the high mountains of the frontier. After contouring round the head of another cirque to 2,152m (7,059ft) Col de Pinata, the path then drops into the Houradade valley where Graham and I camped among the trees. Those seeking a staffed refuge should take the left fork below the Col de Pinata as this leads to the Refuge de Maupas.

The walk is nearly over here as it is only a short stroll down through the woods to the road in the Vallée du Lys, along which you can then walk, or try to hitch a ride, into Luchon. If you have any time left, however, it is worth spending a day on the ascent of 3,109m (10,198ft) Pic de Maupas. From the Houradade, you need first to ascend to the Refuge de Maupas which lies above a téléphérique and an ugly pipeline. From the hut cairns, sparse in places, lead up rock terraces and then granite slabs beside the tiny Maupas glacier to the north-east ridge which is then followed to the summit. A huge pyramid of iron tubing marks the top. The views are good with the steep north face of the nearby 3,116m (10,220ft) Pic des Crabioules especially impressive. The ascent makes an excellent final flourish to the walk as you can look over the wide sweep of the wild mountainous country through which you have travelled, before starting the final descent.

ROUTE

Distance		Place	Elevation	
[km]	[miles]		[metres]	[feet]
0.0	0.0	Bagnères-de-Luchon	650	2,132
6.0	3.5	Hôtel de Superbagnères	1,804	1,120
14.0	8.5	Hourquette des Hounts-Secs	2,275	1,413
16.0	10.0	Refuge d'Espingo	1,967	6,452
18.0	11.0	Coume de l'Abesque	2,099	6,885
22.0	13.5	Port d'Oo	2,908	9,538
26.0	16.0	Valle de Estos	1,860	6,101
35.0	21.5	Puente de Cuera	1,200	3,936
38.0	23.5	Benasque	1,138	3,733
52.0	32.5	Plan d'Estanys	1,870	6,134
55.0	34.0	Port de Venasque	2,444	8,016
63.0	39.0	Cirque de la Glère	1,586	5,202
65.0	40.5	Col de Sacroux	2,034	6,672
67.0	41.5	Col de Pinata	2,152	7,059
69.0	43.0	Refuge de la Coume	1,714	5,622
72.0	44.5	Plan du Lis	1,150	3,772
84.0	52.0	Bagnères-de-Lucon	650	2,130

The ascent of Pico de Posets involves 14km (8¾ miles) and 1,515m (4,969ft) of ascent, the ascent of Pico Aneto 12km (7½ miles) and 1,500m (4,920ft) and the ascent of Pic de Maupas 12km and 1,400m (4,592ft) of ascent.

From Bagnères-de-Lucon, take the road for the Hôtel de Superbagnères but leave this soon afterwards for the waymarked GR10 which climbs the hairpins of an old bobsleigh track to rejoin the road near the hotel. Continue south-westwards on the GR10 across the southern slopes of the Pic de Cécire to the Col de la Coume de Borg. Then cut across the valley heads to the north of the Pic de Subescale and

Pic de Coume Nère to the Hourquette des Hounts-Secs, from where the path descends south-west to the Refuge d'Espingo. The route (now the HRP) turns south here to climb past Lac Saussat into the Coume de l'Abesque. Here the main path is left for a cairned route climbing west of south past the Lac Glace to the Port d'Oo.

From the pass, descend by the easiest route (some cairns) into the Valle de Estos, which is followed on a good path to the Puente de Cuera, and the road which leads south-west to Benasque. This road also takes the route on in a north-east direction from the Puente de Cuera up the Esera valley where it turns into a dirt track, still negotiable by car. In the flat pastureland of the Plans d'Estany, turn north up the path to the Port de Venasque and then descend steeply past the tiny Refuge de Venasque into the Sajust woods. Less than a kilometre from the Hospice de France, turn westwards on a path that traverses the hillside into the Cirque de Glère and then climbs steeply up to the Col de Sacroux, from where a brief descent and ascent leads to the Col de Pinata. The final descent now ensues past the Refuge de la Coume to the roadhead at the Plan du Lis. Luchon lies 12km down the road.

MAPS

Carte de Randonnées 1:50,000 No. 5 Luchon. Editorial Alpina 1:25,000 Posets. Editorial Alpina 1:25,000 Maladeta-Aneto.

TRAIL GUIDES

Battagel, Arthur, *Pyrenees East* (Gaston West Col)
Reynolds, Kev, *Walks and Climbs in the Pyrenees* (Cicerone Press)

Enchanted Mountains, Accursed Mountains:
Salardu to Bagnères-de-Luchon

> *Those days are worthy days that lead through little-known country, unsung and empty of anything but the glory of wild mountain landscapes.*
>
> Kev Reynolds
> **'Astride the Frontier', from Trekking: Great Walks of the World**

South of the Vall d'Aran lies a tangled, complex, wild area of rugged granite mountains; an area of a myriad lakes, a myriad hidden cirques, a myriad rock spires. These are the Sierra de los Encantados, the Enchanted Mountains, a fairyland of harsh yet delicate rock architecture softened by the presence of water and green patures. The area is named for Els Encantats, distinctive peaks which lie on the south-eastern edge of the area in the

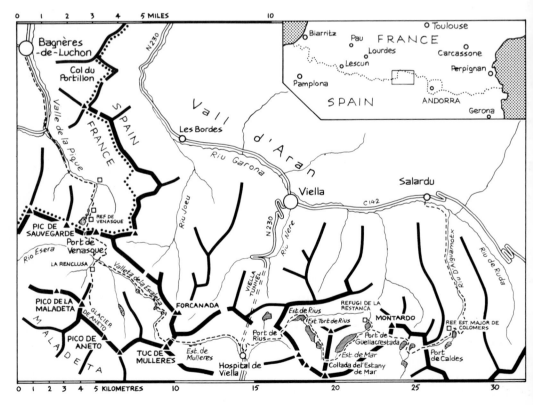

Aigues Tortes-San Maurici National Park. This walk, however, stays north and west of the Encantats and passes through the lovely uplands of the Western Encantados before descending into the deep valley of the Rio Noguera Ribagorzana, which separates them from the darker, bleaker peaks of the Mullères (Moulières) ridge. This is crossed by a high pass, the 2,928m (9,604ft) Coll de Mullères, and the land of the Maladetta, Montagnes Maudites – the Accursed Mountains, entered. The name, it appears, is the result of confusion, Maladetta being a corruption of the local Mala Eta which means no more than 'the highest', which is appropriate as the range contains the highest summit in the Pyrenees, Pico de Aneto. The more romantic, if incorrect, name seems to have been bestowed by one of the earliest Pyrenean pioneers, Ramond de Carbonnières, who came here in 1787 and mistook Mala Eta, which is Spanish, for the Italian Maladetta, hence Monts Maudits.

The walk described here descends from the Mullères ridge into the Valleta de la Escalata to pass between the main Maladetta massif and the frontier peaks before crossing the latter by the Port de Venasque and reaching Luchon by way of the Hospice de France. The heart of the route, from the roadhead in the Aiguamotx valley to the road at the Pont de Ravi, is only 60km (37¼ miles) long. Even so, it will take most walkers a minimum of four days to complete, and long days at that, as the way is rough and the route complex with many high passes to cross. While there are some good paths, for most of the time sketchy trails and the occasional cairn are the best you can expect, even though the line of the HRP is followed, so confidence in your ability with map and compass is required. The ruggedness and steepness of much of the terrain also means this is a walk for those who like easy scrambling and

negotiating rough slopes. In particular, the crossing of the Mullères ridge involves a long (1,300m/4,264ft), steep climb into increasingly rocky country, ending with a scramble to a narrow, rocky arête and a steep pathless descent. Route-finding is as much by eye as mapwork here and this section is perhaps best avoided if the weather is bad.

At either end of the walk, there are road sections that can be avoided by the use of a car or taxi or perhaps at least shortened by hitch-hiking. If these are walked and some of the possible side-trips and ascents taken up, then a week or more could easily be taken for this trek. Pico de Aneto could be climbed during this walk but it fits in better with the Tour de Luchon trek described in the previous chapter where details of what is involved will be found.

Accommodation is available every night if required as there are a number of staffed huts on or near the route as well as the Hospice de Viella in the Noguera Ribagorgana valley. However, even more than on the other walks I recommend camping, for on this route delectable sites present themselves round every corner. If you used even half of them the walk would take a month or more! As no mountaineering equipment is needed, there being no glaciers or snowfields on the route (though there could be snow on the Coll de Mullères early in the season and you would need such gear if Aneto was to be climbed), the weight of camping gear is less of a burden on this walk than on some of the others.

The route starts in the attractive medieval Spanish village of Salardu in the Vall d'Aran to the east of Viella (buses run from France along the N230 road to the latter town). Salardu has picturesque, narrow winding streets, interesting old buildings and a fine church and it is worth spending half a day exploring. More practically, there are grocery stores (stove fuel, even Camping Gaz cartridges, and slide film were not available in 1986, though), restaurants and accommodation. Apart from several hotels, there is a refuge, the Rosta, near the main square and a CEC hut, the Xalet Soler i Santalo, just outside the town on the road to Tredos. A basic camp site can also be found in the fields to the south. If you are looking for a good dinner before heading off into the mountains be warned, though. The food is excellent but the restaurants do not open until 9 p.m.!

From Salardu the route heads south along the tarmac road up the Riu d'Aiguamotx valley. Although the scenery is beautiful, 13km (8 miles) is a long way on a hard surface and those with a car may wish to drive this section and leave their vehicle at the roadhead at the end of the valley. As you then have to come back and collect it, it would perhaps be better to take a taxi along the valley if you do not want to walk it; this is what Alain Kahan and I did. In 1986 the cost was 3,000 pesetas. The road is left where it crosses the stream and curves to the right for a steep switchbacking climb through shrubs and trees, on which we were glad of the extensive cloud cover and cool breeze that prevailed at the start of our walk. It eventually reaches the Estany Major de Colomers. The rubbish from the building of its dam is sadly all too in evidence before the concrete edifice itself is seen. A wardened CEC hut, the Refugi de Colomers, decorates the shores of the lake.

The walk through the Western Encantados can really be said to start at the Colomers lake; unspoilt, wild and beautiful country stretches all the way to the road in the Conangles valley on the far side of the range. A stream is followed west from the lake up a valley and past a small tarn to the first of the many passes on the walk, the grassy saddle of 2,550m (8,364ft) Port de Caldes. We arrived here in thick mist having seen little since the Colomers lake, but as we reached the skyline the sky began to clear to give us first glimpses and then suddenly complete views of the rugged mountain walls of the cirque below us, the peaks dissolving and solidifying in the swirling white air. From the pass, a trace of a path marked by intermittent cairns leads down through the granite boulders to the bright blue Estany de Mengades by whose outlet we camped on a near perfect site with soft turf beneath us and spectacular views all around. To the east, south of the Port de Caldes, can be seen the tower of the Agulles de Travessany, while to the south-west is the long serrated ridge of Besiberri, the major mountain of the Western Encantados with four 3,000m (9,840ft) summits, the highest being 3,032m (9,945ft) Pic de Coma lo Forno at the southern end. Most of these can be climbed by fairly easy scrambling routes (generally Alpine grade PD) from a camp by the Mengades lake or elsewhere in this basin, or from the CEC Refugi Ventosa y Calvell which lies a few kilometres to the south. A tiny basic shelter, the Refugi de Besiberri, lies on the ridge of that name for those who want to spend a night out on the mountain itself.

Horses were grazing on the bright green sward nearby as we sat outside the tent staring at the mountain and dining on pasta flavoured with packet soups. The sky at dusk was still cloudy but at 3.30 a.m. I was woken by the bright light of a full moon, low in the sky to the south, shining on my face through the open tent door. Outside, the rocks glowed yellow and a slight frost lay palely on the grass. At 8 a.m. the sun was just skimming the rocks. Shafts of grey light slanted across the cold granite cliffs to touch others, rendering them a delicate pink – a magic place, a magic dawn. At 8.15 the sun struck the tent and the temperature leapt almost instantly from 6° to 11°C (43° to 52°F). It was time to pack up and move on.

From the Estany de Mengades a gentle

The Lac d'Ansabère.

Descending towards the north face of the Vignemale from the Col des Mulets.

The frontier peaks seen over the Aspe valley.

Camping on the Oulettes des Garbes below the north face of the Vingemale.

A cascade on the Rio Arazas.

Alain Kahan and Mark Edgington crossing the Rio Arazas with the Tozal del Mallo towering above.

Looking from the Faja de Pelay up the Circo de Cotatuero to the south side of the Cirque de Gavarnie with the gash of the Brèche de Roland prominent.

Entering the Vallée de Pouey Aspe.   *Mark Edgington beside the Rio Ara.*

Monte Perdido at dusk.

Monte Aruebo and the dark curve of the Ordesa Canyon from the slopes of Monte Perdido.

Mark Edgington looking north-east to the Neouveille from the summit of Le Taillon.

View across the Cirque de Gavarnie from Le Taillon. The skyline peaks from left to right are Pic de Marbore, Cilindro and Monte Perdido. The top of the Grande Cascade can be seen centre and the Doigt rock pillar bottom right.

Camping in the Vallée de Pouey Aspe with the snow-covered peak of Pimene in the background.

Alain Kahan and Mark Edgington ascending the Vallée de Coubous.

Graham Huntington in the mouth of the Vallée de Pouey Aspe with September snow on the peaks.

The Lacs de Madamète on the climb to the Col de Madamète.

Alain Kahan and Mark Edgington on the Hourquette de Heas.

View from the Plateau de Cardous over the Gavarnie valley to the Vingemale.

Entrance to the Neouvielle Nature Reserve at the Col de Madamète.

Camping in the Vallée de Estos.

Graham Huntington climbing up the Coma de la Paul.

View west from Pico de Aneto; just left of centre can be seen the Pico de Posets, in the distance to the right of it is the Vingemale.

Looking down to the Estany Tort de Rius from the Collada de l'Estany de Mar.

The Refuge de Venasque.

Salardu.

Alain Kahan descending the Valleta de la Escaleta below the twin peaks of the Forcanada.

Camp by the Estany Tort de Rius.

Camp below the Collada del Meners.

Alain Kahan on the climb out of the Vall Ferrera.

Camp below the Etang de Medecourbe.

Pausing for a cool drink during a steep climb.

Sunset over the Pic de St-Barthelemy from a camp below the Crête des Genibres.

Foothill country along the GR10 near the Refuge des Clarans.

Walker descending the Arties valley.

View through the window of a ruined farmhouse on the descent to Siguer.

View from the tent at the camp by the Etang de la Goueille.

View south over the Etang des Dougnes.

Looking down the south ridge of Pic Peric to the Lac des Bouillouses.

The author on the ascent to the Porteille d'Orlu.

Pic Carlit from the Etang des Fourats with the path up the scree gully clearly seen.

On the summit of Montardo.

climb mostly on grass leads past the Estany de Monges (more camp sites here) to the 2,475m (8,118ft) Port de Guellicrestada. Here I left Alain and the packs and, taking just my windshirt, cameras and bumbag, climbed north along the ridge to the 2,830m (9,282ft) Montardo d'Aran, a fine rocky peak with a superb view across the granite and grass-dappled Encantados, shining with water, west to the distant snowy Maladetta and Posets peaks. Right round the horizon, hills fade into the purple distance making this a diversion from the route I highly recommend, if the weather is clear. I shared this splendour with two others and a Catalan flag that decorated the breezy summit. I was back at the pass in an hour, having spent thirty minutes on the ascent, fifteen on the summit and fifteen on the descent.

A well-cairned route leads down from the pass through boulders to the Estany de Cap de Port, at the western end of which a path appears that descends steeply to the Estany de Restanca and the small staffed FCM Refugi de Restanca. Here, if the weather is bad and you do not have the time to sit it out in the hut or your tent, a short-cut can be taken along the upper Arties valley to the Estany Rius. This is a straightforward route avoiding any high passes. The rather more tortuous but far more spectacular main route takes the good path heading south-west of the hut to skirt the brilliant blue waters of the Estany de Mar. Immediately to the south lie the steep walls, small snowfields and jagged ridge of Besiberri. There are many good sites by the lake and when we passed a red tunnel tent at its foot we were half-tempted to stop ourselves even though it was only early afternoon. The path from the lake to 2,468m (8,095ft) Collada de l'Estany de Mar is steep and rocky, climbing through the broken crags by tight little switchbacks. To the south-east there are excellent views of some rock spires; then from the pass itself, a wonderful panorama appears as you look along the complex topography of the white granite boulder-strewn valley which contains the Estany Tort de Rius and the Estany de Rius surrounded by long mountain ridges and rocky peaks – enchanted mountains indeed.

Cairns lead down into the wide valley which, although very rocky, offers many grassy camp sites. We camped at the head of the Estany de Tort Rius – 'a brilliant site', I wrote in my journal. The route, amply marked by cairns, traverses the lakes on their eastern side. This is a rugged walk, as you have to thread a way between the vast number of boulders and slabs that litter the terrain or else scramble over them where no easier route can be found. The actual distance walked is probably twice the length of the valley. The lovely surroundings more than make up for the slow and difficult progress, however. This is not a place to hurry through. At the Estany de Rius there is a magnificent view down the long Vall d'Arties, up which the shorter alternative route comes, with, when we were there, the series of long ridges that dip down into this valley silhouetted in different shadow shades against the sun as they faded away to the horizon.

Shortly past the lake the Port de Rius is reached and a view opens up, across the deep valley of the Noguera Ribagorgana, of the wild

Pico de Aneto from the Coll de Mullères.

and steep Mullères valley rising to a high stony mountain crest that has to be crossed. From here the climb looks daunting, being clearly both long and arduous. At one's feet the Vall de Conangles drops away into the forest below. The path heads down into this and soon the rugged grandeur of the Encantados is exchanged for the gentler beauty of pine then beech woods. This tranquil interlude is soon smashed by the ugly roar and petrol stench of the traffic speeding along the Viella road, the concrete mouth of whose tunnel can be seen rammed into the hillside not far up the valley. Beside this modern highway stand the ancient buildings of the Hospice de Viella. In 1986 this was undergoing renovation and was partially closed but could still offer us bread and cheese and cola for lunch. Normally, accommodation and more extensive meals are available.

The 1,300m (4,264ft) climb to the Mullères ridge comes next, a lengthy ascent through ever more rugged and difficult terrain that we decided to split over two days by camping high in the Mullères valley. From the Hospice, the path winds through more pleasant woodland and pastureland beside the Mullères stream before starting the more serious climb into the granite wilderness above. There is little trace of a path but in places cairns lead upwards round rock bands and small crags. If you cannot find these in places it is fairly easy to make your own way up – just ensure you stay to the right of the stream. Eventually, a stepped series of four cirques, each containing a tarn, is reached. We camped by the lowest of these four Estany de Mullères right on the lip of the cirque, a spectacular site from which we could look across the deep trench where the hospice lay hidden to the now distant upsurge of the Encantados. Snow banks feed these tarns and keep the vegetation between the rock outcrops lush and rich, and when I wandered round the cirque in the cooling dusk

I found hundreds of flowers. Black Redstarts and pipits darted round the meadows, while overhead Ravens soared above the rock wall of the Mullères ridge. On top of a small rise above the lakes I could see people outside a small orange-painted metal shelter. This sleeps twelve and could be useful for those travelling without a tent if the weather were too severe for comfortable bivouacking.

From the lake, the climb to the ridge is long and steep and all on rock, whether huge slabs or small boulders or barren scree. Cairns mark the way in places but cannot be relied on. As the upper lake is approached, the route starts to swing to the right to avoid the cliffs that rise above it, a curve that is continued until you reach the base of the shattered final wall which initially looks impassable. We reached the knife-edge ridge above by a very steep, loose and narrow gully scramble which required the use of hands and which was strenuous and awkward with bulky loads. Whether this is the easiest way through these last cliffs I do not know as there are signs that other gullies have also been used for the ascent. Whichever way is chosen, however, it will be steep and difficult and will require great care.

Once on the ridge, turn left (south) and scramble along the rocky arête a short way to the lowest point (at 2,928m/9,604ft). This is called the Coll de Mullères though it is no more than a slight dip in the arête. Not far to the south lies the 3,010m (9,873ft) summit of the Tuc de Mullères, an even better viewpoint than the col, so it is worth leaving packs on the ridge and making the easy ascent of this peak. After all, you have done the hard part in reaching the ridge. The vista is extensive and impressive. In particular, the Maladetta massif stands out with the summit pyramid of the Pico de Aneto seen clearly above its skirt of glistening glaciers. On my climb of the peak I had to pick my way through a large contingent of the Spanish army who were sitting in full battledress with rifles beside them all over the rocks around the summit, drinking wine. This rather detracted from the grandeur so I did not linger at the peak for very long.

The initial descent is steep and there are likely to be some snow banks to circumvent, but it soon eases off as some massive but gently inclined granite slabs interspersed with dark, silent and chilly looking pools are crossed. Cairns again mark the way. Above rises the distinctive double peak of the 2,881m (9,450ft) Pico Forcanada which can be climbed via the Coll Alfred on the ridge between it and the Coll de Mullères by a PD graded route. A rope is advised for this ascent. As the Valleta de la Escaleta is entered, a path appears which leads down beside a stream to the flat pastures of the Plan Aiguallut. The walk is now easy and relaxing as the path passes through groves of trees and more meadows with plenty of places for pitching a tent. When the junction with the path that leads up to the Renclusa hut is reached, many tents appear as the end of the paved road up the Esera valley lies here, and it is a popular spot for car-based campers. Indeed, so many people do come here that there is a small somewhat rustic store-cum-snack-bar close by.

From this point on, the route coincides with the final stages of that described in the previous chapter (the Tour of Luchon walk) as it crosses the Port de Venasque and descends into France. Alain and I had been over this pass five years previously on that walk but we could not remember whether there were water sources on the climb or not. Having come from the camp in the Mullères valley, we were ready to stop for the day but felt very reluctant to camp with the crowds and cars by the road. As we knew the path crossed some flat areas where a tent could be pitched, we took the risk that there would be water available and

headed wearily upwards. We were wrong. There is no water to be found on or near the ascent and we were forced to extend our long day, cross the narrow notch of the 2,448m (8,029ft) pass (*see* last chapter for details of the view and the easy ascent of Pic de Sauvegarde) and descend to the one-roomed simple Refuge de Venasque and its attendant lakes. The hut being empty when we arrived, we settled inside, but by 9 p.m. there were twelve bodies crammed into its dark confines. By 11 p.m. there were only eleven, though – I had hauled my sleeping bag and mat outside to sleep under the stars, moon, drifting clouds and ring of black peaks as I was unable to settle in the overheated, stuffy hut whose air was permeated with the aroma of sweat and dirty clothing. Outside I slept well, waking at 7 a.m. to find mist all around and my bag damp. It felt strange to lie there, warm and comfortable in my pile cocoon, while wisps of wet cloud settled on my face and drops of moisture hung in the air.

By the time we left at 9 a.m. it was pouring with rain and the mist was even denser. Wearing full waterproofs for the first and only time on the trek, we sloshed down the winding path to the Hospice de France. The walk could be extended by taking the path west from the Pont de Penjat just before the hospice to reach Luchon via the Vallée du Lys, as described in the previous chapter. On this trip, however, Alain and I took the direct route from the hospice along the old decaying flower-lined road, abandoned owing to several landslips, through the misty forest in the Vallée de la Pique. Five kilometres (3 miles) from Luchon the road from Superbagnères is reached at the Pont de Ravi and it may be possible to hitch a ride back into the opulence of Luchon. Or, of course, if you cannot face this, you could turn up the Vallée du Lys and head back into the mountains for a few more days or weeks of reality.

Alain Kahan looking to the frontier peaks from the Coll de Mullères.

ROUTE

Distance		Place	Elevation	
[km]	[miles]		[metres]	[feet]
0.0	0.0	Salardu	1,270	4,166
13.0	8.0	start of path	1,970	6,462
16.0	10.0	Estany Major de Colomers	2,100	6,888
20.0	12.5	Port de Caldes	2,550	8,364
24.0	15.0	Port de Guellacrestada	2,475	8,118
27.0	17.0	Refugi de la Restanca	2,111	6,924
31.0	19.5	Collado de l'Estany de Mar	2,468	8,095
35.0	21.5	Estany de Rius	2,300	7,544
41.0	25.5	Hospice de Viella	1,626	5,333
49.0	30.5	Coll de Mullères	2,928	9,604
56.0	35.0	Plan de Aiguallut	2,050	6,724
62.0	38.5	Port de Venasque	2,444	8,016
66.0	41.0	Hospice de France	1,385	4,543
72.0	44.5	Pont de Ravi	865	2,837
77.0	48.0	Luchon	650	2,132

From the village of Salardu in the Vall d'Aran, the route follows the road up the Aiguamotx valley for 13km (8 miles) to the head of the valley where a path heads up the slopes above to the Refugi de Colomers and the Estany Major de Colomers. Heading west now, the route climbs to the Port de Caldes, then drops down rough slopes to the Estany de Mengades and the Estany de Monges before reascending to the Port de Guellacrestada. Cairns lead down to the Estany de Cap de Port and then on to the Estany de la Restanca and the little Refugi de la Restanca. Turning south-west, the path traverses the eastern shore of the long Estany de Mar before climbing to the Collado de l'Estany de Mar, where it heads north-west to follow the boulder-strewn shores of the Estany Tort de Rius and the Estany de Rius to the Port de Rius.

Here, a long, steep descent ensues down the Vall de Conagles to the Hospice de Viella by the road in the Noguera Ribagorgana valley. An even longer and steeper ascent leads out of the valley due west past the Estany de Mullères to the Coll de Mullères. Heading north-west now, the route descends granite slabs into the Valleta de la Escaleta beneath the Maldetta massif to level out at the Plan de Aiguallut and then follows the valley to the start of the climb up to the Port de Venasque. A final descent leads past the Refuge de Venasque and to the Hospice de France and the abandoned road to the Pont de Ravi, where the paved road into Luchon is joined.

MAPS

Editorial Alpina 1:40,000 Vall d'Aran, Editorial Alpina 1:25,000 La Ribagorca–Montardo, 1:25,000 Maladeta–Aneto. Carte de Randonnées 1:50,000 Luchon.

TRAIL GUIDES

Reynolds, Kev, *Walks and Climbs in the Pyrenees* (Cicerone Press)
Veron, Georges, *Pyrenees High Level Route* (Gaston West Col)

Across Andorra from East to West:

L'Hospitalet to Tabescan

> *Here, between the petrol fumes of the valleys and the snow and ice where only the climber can go, is a much wider region crossed by little-used tracks, sometimes linked by pathless or sparsely waymarked stretches, through which a backpacker may travel the length of a great mountain range or even pass from country to country.*
>
> **Showell Styles**
> *Backpacking in Alps and Pyrenees*

Food bought, gear packed, packs shouldered, we embarked upon the endless tedium of long-distance mechanical travel; a muddled mix of train snacks, British Rail coffee, London rain, underground crowds, channel ports, ferry cafeteria coffee, paperback books, drunks on the ferry, sharp salt sea air in the dark night, passports, French railway coffee, Paris at dawn, a taxi to the wrong station – 'I thought you could speak French, Alain?', 'So did I' – the right train just, seven hours to go, more coffee, more snacks, why on earth are we doing this? Outside the windows towns come and go, fields flash past, hills dark with forest, silvery rivers, red-roofed farms; all are glanced at numbly then ignored. Suddenly, unbelievably, it is L'Hospitalet and we alight, stiff and sore and sleepy, into the harsh sunlight. A

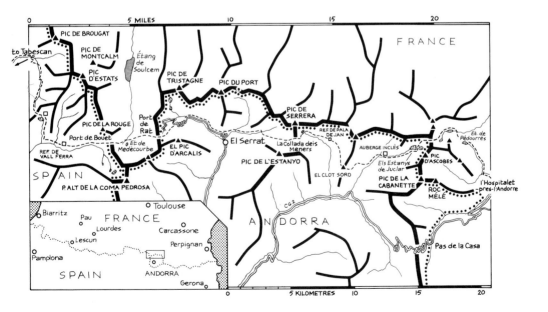

look up and we know why we are here. The Pyrenees. An hour and a half, three kilometres and four hundred and fifty metres of ascent later and the tedium of the journey is forgotten as we make camp at the head of a wild and beautiful valley sheltered by peaceful mountains. The real journey has begun.

L'Hospitalet lies on the direct Paris-Toulouse-Barcelona railway line at a height of 1,436m (4,710ft) and is ideally situated for treks in the eastern Pyrenees. To the east lies the Carlit massif (see 'A Tour of the Carlit'), while to the west lies the land-locked country of Andorra. This tiny land, a co-principality under joint French/Spanish sovereignty, has an area of just 465 square kilometres (180 square miles) and a population of only 33,000. Most of that area is mountainous, rugged terrain split by the long Valira valley which runs south-west from the French border to the Spanish border and in which lies the busy capital, Andorra-la-Vella. By all accounts, this valley is highly developed and to be avoided by the lover of wilderness solitude, although ringing this central thoroughfare are mountains that still retain a feeling of remoteness and peace. How long this will remain so as the tentacles of ski- and road-borne tourist developments creep up the lesser valleys is open to question, but at the time of writing the high country away from the central valley is still worth exploring by those who do not want the mountains made safe and accessible and made into a pretty backdrop for viewing from coach windows, hotel verandas and ski-resort chairlifts.

After due study of the maps and trail guides, Alain Kahan and I had planned a route from L'Hospitalet along various alternatives of the HRP through the northern reaches of Andorra and then, after a brief excursion into France, through Spanish hills and valleys to the village of Tabescan from where taxis can be caught to the larger town of Llavorsi and the road

through the Port de Bonaigua to the Vall d'Aran and then into France (there are bus services along this road to Viella). Alternatively, the walker could continue west from Tabescan to link up with the route described in the previous chapter or else turn north then east to join the one described in the next chapter. But that is a decision to be made when this trek is completed.

Although the walking is generally easy with no scrambling involved or snowfields to cross, paths are often sketchy or non-existent so care with navigation is needed. While there is some accommodation along the way, camping is necessary as what shelter there is available is widely spaced and quite likely to be full. The walk can be done in four days, though taking a few more would be wise as there is much ascent involved and plenty of opportunity for side-trips. Also, as virtually all the route lies south of the frontier with France the weather is likely to be very hot, especially in mid-summer, hardly conducive to fast walking but rather to long lazy afternoons wandering round high camp sites.

Walking straight into the mountains from the train is a delight but it is wise not to plan on going very far the first day, especially as the route starts, inevitably, with an ascent. From L'Hospitalet, which has bar-restaurants but not shops, a path climbs north-westwards up the Sisca valley beside a hydro-electric pipeline under which it passes several times before turning north into the Baldarques valley. Our camp, after just three kilometres (1⅓ miles), was in this valley on the flat Jasse Planel de Roux. It was a peaceful site on a shelf near the stream well away from the path and also out of sight and sound of the busy valley we had left so recently. Although we were camped at 1,900m (6,232ft) and the sky was clear, the temperature only fell to 10°C (50°F) overnight.

By 10 a.m. the next morning it was 24°C

Alain Kahan on the climb out of the Vall Ferrara.

(75°F) and we set off thankful for the cooling effect of a slight breeze. Even so, our cotton sun hats, not an item I usually wear, were essential. By soaking them in cold stream water they worked well at keeping our heads cool. The first part of the continuing ascent up the Baldarques valley is quite gentle as the pretty Etang de Pedourres is bypassed. From that lake, though, the terrain becomes ever more rugged and rocky and wild at each rise and the climb becomes steeper. The path winds a way through boulders and grassy hollows up narrow valleys past the Etang de Couart and Etang de l'Albe to reach the Franco-Andorran border at the 2,539 (8,328ft) Col de l'Albe and a view of the frontier peaks to the west. In less than a kilometre, 2,442m

(8,010ft) la Collada de Juclar, also on the international frontier, is reached. To the north of this pass can be seen the Juclar lakes and the valley up which the Tour of the Haute Ariège (*see* next chapter) trek comes to briefly coincide with this route in the other direction from the Collada de Juclar to the Etang de Couart.

On this walk, however, we descend south-west into Andorra from the col to the two Estanys de Juclar between which the route passes. The good path then continues down the valley below the lakes to the road in the Vall d'Incles where there is a popular camp site and a bar-restaurant where supplies might be obtained as well as drinks and meals. Backpackers who prefer solitude, though, may, as we did, wish to stop before the car campers are reached and seek a quieter site more in keeping with the feelings of remoteness and wilderness engendered by the day's walk. We pitched our tent by the Rill de Juclar about a kilometre before the road is reached on a flower-, pine- and stream-strewn shelf below shattered granite boulder slopes topped by cliffs – a fine site. Of course, you could stop sooner (or have a longer first day) and camp at one of the lakes earlier in the walk and deeper in the mountains. We saw several tents pitched by these.

Again, the calm night was warm, 10°C (50°F) being the lowest the thermometer reached, with a starry sky and a very heavy dew that made it worth while using the tent, though we did leave the doors open so we could lie and watch the stars shining above the dark edge of the hills. Remembering the heat of the previous day, we made an earlier start, quickly dropping into the Vall d'Incles and past the camp site and then much more slowly ascending the steep, wooded slopes to the north-west. There is not much of a path on this climb and when the sun is out it is a sweaty, airless haul so it was with relief that we left

A *typical* hostal.

the pines for the gentler grassy slopes and the small Estanyo del Querol, even though the views down the Incles valley were good. Still on grass, the spur running down from the frontier ridge to the Clot Sord is crossed just to the north of the latter minor peak.

Once over this crest, a long up and down traverse on an unclear, intermittent path above the Vall de Ransol ensues. The head of this long wooded valley passed, the still minimal path climbs right under the walls of the frontier peaks, skirts a couple of tarns and then ascends the final slopes to the narrow notch of the 2,713m (8,900ft) Collada dels Meners (Col de la Mine) which lies on the subsidiary ridge running south from the Pic de Serrara on the frontier and the Pic de la Cabaneta to the south. The climb of the latter peak looks feasible from the pass, though I have not tried to do it. There is also an alternative high-level route to the Collada del Meners from the Vall d'Incles that I have not done, which looks interesting though which is clearly tougher than the one described. Veron describes it as 'for mountaineers and fine weather only'. Briefly, it climbs out of the valley to the summit of the Pics de la Portaneille, then follows the frontier to the Port de la Coume d'Ose (Collado de Jan) from where it descends to join the route as described a kilometre or so before the Collada del Meners.

The views from the Collada del Meners are excellent but on our crossing they also revealed black clouds building up over the frontier peaks to the north, so we did not linger but made a hasty descent as the first rumbles of thunder echoed round the peaks. We found a small site by the stream just as the rain began and were soon brewing up in the shelter of the tent. Our camp was just above the first trees and only four kilometres (2½ miles) from the little village of El Serrat. The sky cleared within half an hour, the storm moving off elsewhere, and by 9 p.m. the temperature was back up to 16°C (61°F) though for the third night running it fell to 10°C (50°F) overnight. Although the site was chosen because of the weather, it was another scenic one with good views of the mountains to the west.

The next morning we wandered down the pleasant path through the forest and past the large, apparently unstaffed, Borda de Sortany hut to the road, which we left after a short stretch for an old path that descended by the stream into El Serrat. Lying 16 kilometres (10 miles) up the Valira de Nord from Andorra-la-Viella, this hamlet, no more than a collection of farm buildings and hotels, is a popular destination for tourists and all accommodation is likely to be booked up for the summer so rooms should not be relied upon. There are no shops so you cannot resupply here. We were only interested in what was to offer in the way of food to eat immediately and had a second breakfast of cheese sandwiches and cola in one of the restaurants before heading north-west for the long, hot drag up the road that sadly has been bulldozed into the upper reaches of the Tristaina valley where downhill ski facilities were being constructed in 1986. A steady stream of car and coaches snorted past, belching fumes, so we were grateful to leave the tarmac and make a diversion on an old path that climbed up alongside a refreshing cascade to the attractive if highly popular Tristaina lakes.

An easy link can be made here with the Tour of the Haute Ariège walk described in the next chapter, and the last part of that walk follows back to the railway line at L'Hospitalet or Merens-les-Vals to make a circular route, an alternative worth consider-

ing if you do not want to finish at Tabescan. To make this connection, continue on the path north-east of the lakes that climbs to the Franco-Andorran frontier at the 2,601m (8,531ft) Port de l'Abeille, then descend through broken terrain (no path) to the Etang de la Goueille where the Haute Ariège walk is joined. It is also possible to climb 2,878m (9,440ft) Pic de Tristagne from the lakes (where a tent could be pitched) by an easy scramble, and the 2,903m (9,522ft) Pic du Port from the road a few kilometres above El Serrat also by an easy route (*see* Battagel's *Pyrenees Andorra Cerdange* for details of these ascents).

From the lakes, a wide path (the one used by car-borne tourists) leads quickly to the road which now winds up the valley by a series of hairpin bends. The walker can cut these and head straight upwards over marshy terrain. Finally, the road, intended apparently to reach France eventually via a tunnel at this point, ends and an old, fallen-into-disuse path leads up through rocks away from the despoliation of the ruined valley head to the 2,540m (8,331ft) Port de Rat which lies on the frontier. Andorra has now been crossed from east to west and is here left behind, the remainder of the walk taking place in France, briefly, and Spain.

From the pass, there are excellent views into France and across the head of the Soulcem valley to the wide col of the Port de Bouet where we are heading. Getting there is not as simple as it looks, however. Reaching the valley bottom is straightforward, a good cairned path leading down the mountainside to cut through the loops of the road that climbs to what will presumably be the other end of the tunnel from Andorra. At one point, a rough stone shelter, the Orri de Rat, is passed. From the valley bottom, the slopes leading up to the Port de Bouet look far more complex than they did from the Port de Rat.

Once across the Bareytes stream, ascend slopes covered with alpenroses on a good path.

Now in 1986 we followed this clear cairned path upwards, sure it must be the route to the Port de Bouet, until a lake appeared where a lake should not have been and the path faded away. The map suggested this was probably the Etang de Medecourbe which we knew from the trail guides was not on the route to the pass. As the Carte de Randonnées 1:50,000 Andorre map does not show a route to the Port de Bouet corresponding with that described in the trail guides, we were relying on the latter (it also does not show the good path we had followed). To confirm where we were, I abandoned the packs and Alain and climbed up the steep slopes to the north to a high col. The view showed that we were indeed at the Etang de Medecourbe and in the wrong valley. It being too late to try to correct our error that evening and it being, anyway, a beautiful spot, we camped by the stream below the green waters of the lake. During the evening a sheep tried to eat the tent!

As often happens, we found ourselves and the mislaid route to the Port de Bouet easily enough in the freshness of the morning. All we did was to traverse round the ridge to the north until we intercepted the right path. This must split from the path to the Etang de Medecourbe lower down, a junction we had missed, probably because we were not looking for it. The view from the pass is excellent and extensive from the Andorran peaks to the east and south, to the Spanish ones that lie ahead and the French ones to the north.

From the pass, the route descends west over

The Etang de Baborte and the Coll de Sellente.

The cascades on the climb to the Tristaina lakes.

open slopes where the way is clear, though there is not much of a path until the trees and then the pasture of the Pla de Bouet are reached. Just past the meadows, the waters of the Barranco d'Areste tumble down from the north-east. A very short way up this stream is the small (sixteen-bed) wardened stone-built Refuge de Vall Ferrara. This hut is a good base for ascents of the three easternmost 3,000m peaks of the Pyrenees which lie to the north; 3,143m (10,310ft) Pica d'Estats, 3,077m (10,093ft) Pic de Montcalm and 3,072m (10,076ft) Pic du Port de Sullo. The climbs are not difficult but ice axe and crampons are recommended for both Estats and Montcalm. I have not yet been up these peaks. For those who want to, details will be found in Reynolds' *Walks and Climbs in the Pyrenees*.

Down the valley from the hut, the Noguera de Vall Ferrara is crossed by a bridge, and a long traversing ascent that is very tiring in the grim centre of a hot afternoon takes you up through beautiful woodland on a good, if steep, dry and dusty path. Be warned: there is no water on this ascent. We arrived at the top parched, having foolishly set off with empty water bottles. After levelling out and contouring round the hillside, this path reaches a small shepherd's hut, the Cabane de Basello, perched on the lip of flat pastureland overlooking the green depths of the Vall Ferrara. There is a welcome stream just below the hut. All this is glorious country as is that now entered as the route climbs northwards, no longer on a path, though there are cairns, up steep grass and rock slopes to the beautiful Estany de Baborte above whose northern shore on a little knoll sits a tiny emergency shelter, the Refuge de Baborte. We were glad to find a cool wind blowing off the lake as we made our way round its eastern shore before climbing gently up to the wide 2,485m (8,151ft) Coll de Sellente. Here, surprisingly, it was calm and, not quite so surprisingly, the views were

good, especially those looking back down to the Baborte lake.

After all the cross-country walking we were glad to find not far below the col a good, fast, switchbacking trail that kept improving as it led down, down into deep valleys and then into the woods along the Broate stream and the roadhead at the Planell de Boavi. This is a flat pastureland dotted with small shrubs, birch and spruce where many people camp and picnic in the summer. We camped here, too, impressed by the beauty of the surroundings but dismayed at the damage and squalor left by other campers.

There now remains just a 9km (5½ miles) walk down the road to the little village of Tabescan, a pleasant trek beside the Riu de Lladorre through woods and meadows decorated with picturesque old stone barns. In Tabescan, itself an attractive hamlet with a fine curving stone bridge and interesting old buildings, we lunched on cheese and bread and cola in the cool shade of a bar-restaurant wall before opening up protracted negotiations about transport that ended with us paying 2,000 pesetas for a Land-Rover taxi to Llavorsi where there are supermarkets, banks and other facilities.

The walk starts at the railway station in L'Hospitalet. The path out of the village climbs north-west beside pipelines up the Sisca valley then turns north up the Balderques valley. This is followed to the Etang de Pedourres at its head. The path then traverses the hillsides above the tarn before climbing over a small col to reach the Etang Couart and ascends past a series of tarns to the Etang de l'Albe and then the Col de l'Albe on the Franco-Andorran frontier. Gently descend to the Collada de Juclar, then more steeply to the Estanys de Juclar whose outlet stream is followed (and crossed several times) down to the Vall d'Incles where there is a campsite and bar-restaurant. Descend the road in the valley for about a kilometre then cross the meadows to the north and climb steeply through the forest to emerge on the small flat grassy area just north of the Clot Sord. The path now cuts across the mountainside above the Vall de Ransol, crossing many streams eventually to climb above the head of that valley to the Collada dels Meners. A descent down the valley to the west leads on into forest and then in turn to a road and the village of El Serrat.

The route now ascends the Tristaina valley, occasionally on the road where necessary, and on adjacent paths where possible until the tarmac is eventually left behind for the final climb to the Port de Rat. A good path leads directly down into the Bareytas valley where the stream and road are crossed and the path followed up the Medecourbe is reached, to climb on a zigzag path through rock bands and then over grass and broken rock to the Port de Bouet. Descend from the pass, keeping well above and to the north of the stream below, into the woods to reach the Vall Ferrara and, on the slopes above, the Refugi de Vall Ferrara. From the hut, take the road which goes down the valley a short way to where a path branches right leading to a bridge over the Noguera de Vall Ferrara. Follow this path on a rising traverse through woodland to the small Cabane de Basello. Here turn due north and climb the slopes on a vague, intermittent path to the Baborte lake, which is turned from on its eastern shore and the slopes beyond climbed to the Coll de Sellente. Descend into the bowl below on a clear path that then follows a stream down (north) into woodland through which it winds to the Planell de Boavi and a roadhead. Tabescan lies 9km (6 miles) down this road.

MAP

Carte de Randonnées 1:50,000 Andorre.

ROUTE

Distance		Place	Elevation	
[km]	[miles]		[metres]	[feet]
0.0	0.0	L'Hospitalet	1,436	4,710
5.0	3.0	Etang de Pedourres	2,165	7,101
10.0	6.0	Col d'Albe	2,539	1,577
15.0	9.5	Vall d'Incles	1,875	6,150
18.0	11.0	Clot Sord	2,450	8,036
24.0	15.0	La Collada des Meners	2,713	8,899
31.0	19.5	El Serrat	1,560	5,117
39.0	24.0	Port de Rat	2,540	8,331
41.0	25.5	Baryetes stream	2,000	6,560
43.0	26.5	Port de Bouet	2,520	8,266
47.0	29.0	Refugi de Vall Ferrara	1,940	6,363
53.0	33.0	Coll de Sellente	2,485	8,151
59.0	36.5	Planell de Boavi	1,460	4,789
68.0	42.0	Tabescan	1,100	3,608

TRAIL GUIDES

Battagel, Arthur, *Pyrenees Andorra Cerdagne* (Gaston West Col)
Useful if you wish to climb some peaks along the way.

Reynolds, Kev, *Walks and Climbs in the Pyrenees* (Cicerone Press)

Only the section from El Serrat to Tabescan is covered.

Veron, Georges, *Pyrenees High Level Route* (Gaston West Col)
This covers the whole route plus many alternatives.

A Tour of the Haute Ariège:
From Merens-les-Vals

> The little-known mountains of this region are among the finest and wildest of the Pyrenees . . . ordinary walkers and tourists are not advised to pass this way; there is no continuous path and no effective marking . . . the ground is tricky to follow in misty weather . . . the terrain can also prove difficult in places.
>
> Georges Veron
> **Pyrenees High Level Route**

Passages such as the above are guaranteed to have keen wilderness walkers reaching for their boots and heading off to explore such perfect-sounding places, or at least pulling down maps from their shelves to work out routes. Veron's words certainly grabbed my attention and had me planning a walk to take in as much as possible of this region, the result being the trek described here. The area so emotively referred to is the Haute Ariège which lies west and south of the Ariège valley and north of the frontier with Andorra and Spain in the eastern Pyrenees. Because of the difficult terrain and remoteness of the area, the 'official' HRP runs south of the border here (the route described in the previous chapter follows much of it) but there is a *variante* that stays north of the frontier, while at a lower level the GR10 skirts the northern, forested edge of the mountains. The two routes touch at the Etang Fourcat just north of the northwestern corner of Andorra so I decided to make a circular route by linking the two. The obvious starting point is the Ariège valley itself which cuts deep into the mountains between the Haute Ariège and Carlit ranges and through which runs the Paris-Toulouse-Barcelona railway line. As the route starts and finishes in the little village of Merens-les-Vals which has a station on this line, access to the route is easy.

While this walk should be well within the capabilities of experienced mountain backpackers with good navigational and route-finding abilities, Veron's warnings should be heeded. Even the GR10 has a short section of scrambling on it, while the HRP is only a line on the map, not a path on the ground, and there is much complex, rugged and steep terrain to be crossed. As many long steep-sided ridges stretch north from the frontier, there is much up and down, too, as the route jumps from valley to valley. It is also a long route, requiring at least eight days to walk. Most people will probably want to take longer. Although there are a number of basic shelters along the way, there is only one staffed refuge so this is a walk for the camper. The only supplies available are in Auzat, roughly halfway through the walk, which the GR10 avoids but which most walkers will visit as eight or more day's food is rather too much to carry.

Merens-les-Vals is a pleasant village split by a busy main road. There are a couple of hotels – only one of which serves meals – a small grocery store and a post office. Red and white painted waymarks lead through the houses and past a drinking fountain, where water bottles should be filled as there is a long, dry and steep ascent ahead, to the start of the path up the wooded Mourgouillou valley. I sweated up this path on a baking hot afternoon regretting

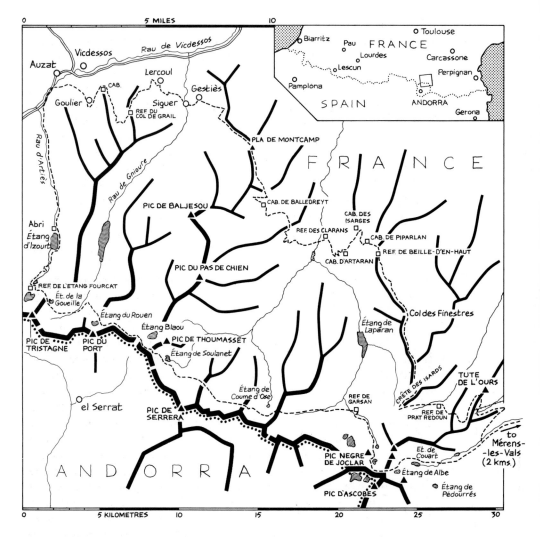

not having filled my water bottle. As soon as the path came close to the stream below, inaccessible owing to steep banks and dense vegetation for most of the climb, I stopped to have a drink. I was in so much of a hurry to quench my thirst that I dropped the cap of my only water bottle into the rushing waters where it quickly disappeared. Cursing, I began to hunt downstream for it, peering under boulders and poking into eddies with my stick. Losing the lid would have been serious as I

knew that there were many long sections between water sources to be walked in the days ahead. After half an hour, though, I had just about given up the search when I found it between two rocks less than a metre from where it fell in. Throughout the search I had been remembering how the same thing had happened just about a year previously in the Canadian Rockies and wondering how I had been stupid enough to let it occur again. Then I had also found it close to where it had been dropped. Doing so again made me feel very lucky and also to resolve to be more careful and to buy a bottle with an attached cap when I replaced this one.

A couple of kilometres up the valley a roadhead with a large area for parking cars is passed, so those with a vehicle could cut out the first part of the climb if they so wished. I had met no one lower down but beyond the road I met many day walkers and picnickers descending. As the terrain starts to level out, the path crosses the stream by the four flat stone slabs of the Pont des Pierres. Four hundred metres (400 yards) further upstream the GR10 branches off from the path up the valley and starts to angle up the hillside to the north-east. There are many pleasant camp sites on the edge of the trees by the stream before this junction and, as there is no guaranteed water for quite a way, this is a good place to stop. I did so, pitching my tent on the far side of the stream from the path in long grass shaded by birch and fir trees. Two other tents soon appeared just downstream. Such sheltered, fairly low-level sites have their disadvantages, though: mosquitoes and biting flies forced me into the tent at dusk despite the temperature of 19°C (66°F).

A dipper bobbing on the rocks in the stream entertained me over breakfast before I set off on the long, hot and sweaty climb on a vague path to the Col du Savis, during which I was harassed by clouds of flies but which also gave good views of the black serrated crest of the Carlit massif to the east and the tiny houses of Merens-les-Vals far below in the valley. At the col the route turns abruptly south of west to pass through the edge of the Saquet ski resort. Although the terrain is rather spoilt by the dirt roads and mechanical uplifts, here the cool water of the Estagnols stream is most welcome as it is the first since the one in the Morgouillou valley. Ski roads lead up from the stream to reach the ridge above at the Couillade de Llerbes. Leaving the ski debris behind, the path traverses across grassy slopes with excellent views south-west to the jagged peaks around the Pic de Ruille and then curves down into the huge grass basin of the Jasse des Llerbes which provides summer grazing for herds of cattle. A gentle climb leads to a col, unnamed on the 1:50,000 map but called the Couillade de Combeille in the topo guide. From this pass a steep descent leads down into the next valleyhead where lies the tiny Refuge de Prat Redon on whose sun-trapping steps I sat and had lunch.

A mostly pathless though quite clear ascent leads from the hut up the Ruisseau du Najar valley to the Col de Beil. The hot, sticky, humid weather continued as I passed through a large herd of cows half-way up the valley, the bells round their necks jangling as they shook their heads to deter the flies. I sympathized, as whenever I paused swarms of flies would gather round my head. Also gathering, however, over the frontier peaks to the south, were large thunder clouds, presaging a break in the weather and hopefully a cooler airstream. At the Col de Beil the GR10 turns northwards along the narrow rocky arête of the Crête des Isards, a good route. I rushed to try this to reach lower ground before the thunder broke. In doing so, I missed the cairned turn off the ridge just before the main peak at the north end and started up the latter only to be turned back by steep slabs and small cliffs near the summit. The actual route runs below the cliffs on the west side on a narrow path that is exposed in parts and on which hands are needed in a few places. The long ridge is followed further north until it is left for the broad grassy slopes which lead west down to the Col de Didorte. There is no path, so care needs to be taken not to overshoot this turning and continue along the ridge towards Ax-le-Thermes.

A few hundred metres past the col, the

route crosses an area of springs ('little ponds' says the topo guide) and tiny streams below the shattered pinnacles of the Crête des Gembres. As the next water lay 6.5km (4 miles) ahead and the 21km (13 miles) I had walked had taken me nearly eight hours, I camped here looking out east from the tent to the Pic d'Espaillat ridge. Continuing rumbles of thunder led to just a few spots of rain but a thankful cooling of the air. Bells echoing round the hills came from a flock of sheep on the far side of the valley. Clouds drifted in from the north-west in the cool of the evening to allow a subtle orange pink sunset to take place, with the Pic de St-Barthelemy to the north hanging alone etched against the sky and the clouds.

During the night a gusty wind swept over the site, waking me to gaze out at a clear starry sky. A tongue of mist licking over the slopes of the Lavail valley to the north early the next morning had me rushing to the lip of this bowl to see the whole valley below white with cloud, with again the Pic de Barthelemy rising above it – a glorious sight. Ten minutes later, though, and the mist was curling round the tent, visibility now no more than a few metres. This soon cleared and I set off in bright sunlight for a marvellous, undulating grassy ridge walk, partly on vehicle tracks, over the bump of Prat Moll to the Plateau de Beille and a large herd of cattle. The Beille d'en Haut shelter here was fenced off (this was July 1989) and obviously uninhabited.

The descent from the plateau into the valley below is the most difficult part of the GR10 section of this walk because of the number of new bulldozed roads that have been

The Refuge des Clarans.

Pic du Port and the Etang du Rouch.

made. Finding no sign of a path or any way-marks, I made my own way downwards through forest and pasture to the Jasse d'Artaran where there is a small unlocked shelter and a fine view over the forest to the hills to the west. I found the path again here, for which I was grateful as there follows a steep, lengthy descent through dense pine then beech forest that would be difficult without a path. At a stream crossing in the forest where I stopped for a drink I met an English walker in a white headscarf with a large pack who was heading upwards. Phil looked sunburned and trail hardened so I was not surprised to learn that he had set off from the Atlantic on a traverse of the Pyrenees thirty-four days earlier. 'I never knew thirty-four days could be so long,' he said, adding that he was thoroughly enjoying the walk and that it would take him

another two weeks to reach the Mediterranean. He had followed the HRP as far as Gavarnie but from there had stuck to the GR10 in order to avoid the glaciers and the more mountainous terrain. He had also sent his ice axe and tent home to save weight and was relying on huts for shelter.

Leaving Phil to continue east (he intended reaching the Prat Redon shelter that day), I finished the descent to the valley, passing on the way down the small Clarans shelter, situated on the edge of a very pretty meadow. At the building of Coudènes a 610m (2,000ft) ascent begins as the path climbs through the beech trees of the Bois de Gudanes near a stream and several attractive waterfalls to enter the Calvière valley. Here I lost the path and went well over a kilometre upstream to the Cabane des Ludines where I realized I had gone too far. Rather than retrace my steps, I continued past the hut and climbed up to the col west of the summit of Massayre. I then crossed this 1,922m (6,304ft) hill to descend to rejoin the proper route at 1,693m (5,553ft) Col de Sirmont, adding a couple of hundred extra metres (600ft) of ascent and five kilometres (3 miles) of distance to walk. To avoid this rather pointless diversion, climb the steep slopes of bracken and rocks that rise to the north soon after the Calvière valley is entered. There does not appear to be a path.

From the col, a steep path leads down through woods to the pretty meadows of the Sirbal valley where there are several good camp sites. Indeed, I considered stopping here and took off my pack but an over-abundance of horse flies soon had me moving again. The climb continues up the Balledreyt valley where I camped by the stream after wandering up the slopes above to look at the Belledreyt shelter where I was considering staying. Sadly, though, what I found was a semi-ruin with holes in the roof, no door, a broken sleeping platform and much garbage scattered on the floor. Luckily there are plenty of good sites in the valley bottom on short grass well-grazed by cattle. From the lip of the valley I sat and watched a slow pink dusk merge into the dark of night. Down below I could see the flickering orange of a camp-fire in the Sirbal valley.

The Balledreyt valley is not as remote as it feels, as you find on the climb to the hill spur known as Courtal Marti. A dirt road cutting across the head of the valley comes into view. Grassy hillsides dotted with herds of cattle are crossed next as the vague path, marked by occasional very faded waymarks, descends to the Col de Sasc and then ascends 1,904m (6,245ft) Pla de Montcamp. From there you drop down to the Col de Gamel and good views of the villages of Siguer below and Lercoul high on the slopes opposite. The

descent to the former is mostly on a narrow track between high banks lined with a tangle of shrubs and small trees and several ruined farmhouses. Watch out for nettles if you descend this path wearing shorts! The sound of a church bell close by signified my arrival in the village of Gesties. Not far below lie the narrow streets of Siguer, a village with a forgotten, indolent air. The topo guide says there is a shop here. There isn't. There is a bar with a friendly owner where I had a couple of drinks but it does not serve meals, though I was sold a baguette from the owner's freezer. The lack of food was a problem as I had planned on both buying supplies for the rest of the walk and having a long and large lunch here.

Consulting the map, I realized that I would have to make a diversion to Auzat, a town I thought I could reach that afternoon if I moved fast. So I was soon climbing the steep, wooded path to the hamlet of Lercoul, perched high on the hillside above Siguer, and then the Crox de Ste-Tanoque where a frame tent was pitched by the minor road that reaches the hillcrest here. Box, hazel, beech and pine trees line the terraced path for the pleasant traverse to the Col de Lercoul and then the Col de Grail. From the last col, a gravel road leads round the head of the Sem valley where there is water in the two stream beds, the first since Siguer, though the terrain is far too steep for camping. Soon the Col d'Esquerus is reached and the GR10 divides into two. For Auzat, take the right-hand branch which leads to the Col de Risoul and down another wooded track to the village of Goulier. From here field paths, marked GR10 in places, can be taken to Auzat where there are good shops, hotels and a rather dusty and, in August at least, crowded camp site. I passed the latter by for a night in a good and inexpensive hotel where the friendly and helpful staff were most concerned that I might

find the set evening meal too rich in garlic (I didn't, I like garlic). The shops in town provided chocolate, granola bars, cheese, coffee and more, but not slide film, just colour prints.

At Auzat the westward section of the walk is complete and the route now turns south to head back towards the high mountains. Between here and the Etang Fourcat is a climb of 1,700m (5,576ft). Spurred on by the very strong coffee served by the hotel at breakfast, I headed up the road to Arties and then Pradières where there is a bar-restaurant with refuge-type accommodation. The tarmac is left soon afterwards at the Pradières electricity

station and the GR10 rejoined for the popular and pleasant walk up to the Etang d'Izourt where there is a shelter in one of the abandoned buildings by the dam. There is a feeling of re-entry to the world of the mountains as the path traverses the east shore of the bright blue lake and then climbs a steep gully in a series of tight switchbacks to the Orri de la Caudière, around which there is plenty of space for camping. Still ascending rapidly, the well-made path next climbs a steep rocky face above a ravine to reach the lower Fourcat lake round which it winds to the staffed Refuge de Fourcat, an old hut in a splendid situation. I continued, however, heading east past the beautiful Etang Fourcat with the high mountains of the frontier ridges towering over it, and via a line of cairns across a gully and a field of boulders to the Etang de la Goueille by which I camped. This is a superb site which on my stay was made even more wonderful by the brilliant evening light over the valleys to the north as the sun crept round the edges of the buttresses of the spur of the Pic de Tristagne that walls the lake to the west. I followed the sun up the hillside with my camera and tripod, shooting a roll of film as the light constantly changed.

The night was starry with a cool breeze. There was also a constant clanging of sheep bells which I thought of as mobile wind chimes! As the tent was facing east the sun was soon shining through the door in the morning and I was off to an early start. The

HRP east of here traverses difficult, pathless terrain. Those who prefer easier ground could head south instead over the Port de l'Albeille to connect with the route across Andorra described in the previous chapter and follow that in reverse back to L'Hospitalet which is on the same railway line as Merens-les-Vals. This would also be a good alternative if the weather were bad. Those continuing with this route should be prepared for slow progress. The day out from the Goueille lake I made just eleven kilometres (7 miles) in 7½ hours of walking.

From the Goueille lake, the route climbs gently to the col to the south-east and then descends into the Gnioure valley where there are traces of a path on the right bank of the stream. Somewhere another path is meant to lead up to the Etang du Rouch high on the

The Etang Blaou.

mountainside to the east, but I could not find this and ended up scrambling up scree gullies and rock terraces that were sometimes too steep for comfort to a flat grassy ridge north of and well above the lake; it looks impressive from here with the fine peak of the Pic du Port rising above the dark waters. Shattered rock pinnacles prevented a direct descent to the lake, so I went down the grass and scree to the east and then contoured round to the col east of the lake. The HRP guide describes the route from this col as contouring across the slopes to the right to the foot of a chimney which is then climbed 'with care'. Frankly, the traverse looked difficult and very exposed as the mountainside here is steep and craggy and the only chimneys I could see looked unclimb-able. This feeling was reinforced by the sight of two people slowly and precariously descend-ing into the top of one of them from the ridge above. I could see no way up those slopes that I was prepared to try with a heavy pack.

The aim at this point is to reach the frontier ridge south-west of the Pic d'Arial. It looked to be easier to do this further to the east so I descended into the cirque below to the first of the many Etangs des Llassies. A good camp could be made in this wild yet grassy-bottomed bowl. Above, a herd of twenty-plus isards scampered over the rocks, making a mockery of human attempts at climbing. From the tarn I climbed straight up the scree and grass above to the ridge, a steep and long but not difficult ascent. It is then just a stroll to the 2,681m (8,794ft) summit of Pic d'Arial from where there are superb views, especially of 2,903m (9,522ft) Pic du Port along the frontier to the west. From the summit, descend to the Port de Siguer where a path goes down west into Andorra and eventually to El Serrat to join the 'Across Andorra' walk (*see* previous chapter).

Our route continues along the frontier which I did rather quickly as huge thunder-heads were building up rapidly to the south and west. Conditions were ideal for a big storm, with a cool breeze blowing up from the north and hot, humid air rising from the south. At the pass I hesitated. What to do? To the north, the green sward by the lovely Etang Blaou looked inviting but I could count ten tents already pitched round its shores and see more people heading that way. Preferring a greater degree of solitude, I took the risk of hurrying on as the thunder began, cutting below the Pic de Bagnels on the Andorran side to the Port de Bagnel ou de Soulanet and a descent to the Etang Soulanet. I camped here, alone in scenic surroundings with the Pic de Thoumasset to the north and the Pic du Mil-Menut away to the east. Alone, that is, except for the usual flock of bell-ringing sheep and a herd of equally noisy cattle lower down the valley.

The storm soon passed, the threat having been more than the performance, and at 8.30 in the evening I set off up the 300 metres (1,000ft) to Pic de Bagnels. A cloudy sky made me wonder if the climb was worth while but something kept me clambering upwards. I am glad it did, as I reached the summit to see the sky and clouds to the west red with a glorious sunset. Below, on one side, camp fires around the Etang Blaou glowed orange while far down the dark valleys of Andorra three sets of white lights shone. I descended carefully in the dark, picking out pale boulders and shades of slope noted on the climb. I did not use my head lamp so as not to ruin my night sight.

During the night a gusty wind brought a little rain, and the sky was cloudy at dawn. As I breakfasted on stewed dried fruit (raisins, bananas and pears) mixed with condensed milk from a tube, the sun started to break through the clouds, for which I was thankful as I knew another day of problematic route-finding lay ahead ('for mountaineers keen on wild, desolate terrain,' says Veron. That's me!). An easy contour led to the Col du Sal from where I descended into the Coume de Seignac; here a farmer was bringing up a herd of cattle and also setting small fires in the grass. I had seen smoke the night before, and now I knew what it was from though the reason for it escaped me. I went too high and then too low on the crossing of the rough back wall of the Coume to the start of the climb to the Col de l'Homme Mort, being forced off my line by small cliffs in several places. It would, I think, be best to aim for the lowest rockband where there is a ruined hut and ascend from there. Two German walkers, complete with *lederhosen*, were descending the scree from the col as I laboured upwards. They said they had come from Andorra over the Col de Coume d'Ose that lies just to the south here and were heading for the Refuge de Quioules that lies well down the Siegnac valley. I then met two people resting at the col and two coming up the scree from the other side. This crossing from Andorra is clearly quite popular.

This route stays in France, though, and descends below the pass to contour for nearly two kilometres around the headwall of the Coume d'Ose at about half-height on very steep slopes of boulders, scree and occasionally grass. There are a few cairns. Once on this traverse you should stay at the same height until it is over, as there are steep slabs and cliffs below. The crossing appears very steep and intimidating from either end but is not as bad as it looks. From the unnamed col on the far side there is a steep descent on grass into the Coume de Varilhes that I imagine could be very treacherous when wet. As I descended, a cacophony of bells rose from the valley bottom where a large herd of black horses and white cows were grazing. A path now appears leading down the valley to the Pla de Lespeyre where I was surprised to see about twenty cars parked and a road coming up the valley; surprised because this road is not marked on the 1986 edition of the 1:50,000 map nor

mentioned in the guidebook. I cut across the grass above the roadhead to reach a good path heading up beside the cascades of the Aston stream; this is crossed by a new metal bridge below the Refuge de Garsan. The path over the stream leads past the Etangs de Fontargente to the Port de Fontargente and down to the Vall d'Incles in Andorra where again the route of the previous chapter is joined.

Wanting, however, to stay north of the frontier, I stayed on the left (true right) bank of the stream and followed it upwards, on a good path not marked on the map, to climb through a mass of flowers, a hanging garden almost, and across an open sloping meadow where a camp could be made, to the unnamed tarns between the magnificent soaring rocky shoulders of Pics Nègre de Juclar and de Ruille, a beautiful spot with little space for camping, in fact just one overused small flat site featuring fire rings and rubbish by the upper tarn. The walls above this tarn to the south look difficult to ascend, if not impassable, but the path leads on up steep scree beside a high cliff, down which tumbles a cascade, to level out on the lip of the cirque holding the Etang de Joclar. Again, there are few flat spots round the rocky shores. Those that there are lie at the south end where I could see four tents already pitched. I managed to find a tiny site just big enough for my small tent among the rocks above and out of sight of the other tents. As I arrived the weather changed to give a gloomy evening with a cool gusting west wind and dark clouds swirling round the pinnacles of the peaks above.

By 7.30 a.m., however, the wind had stilled and the sky was clear. A light dew lay on the ground, and across the cirque the sun was warming the peaks. The final day of the walk looked like being hot. But by the time I set off at 9.30, after a breakfast of butter biscuits and jam, almost the last of my food, the clouds were rolling back in. A cairned path leads to

The cascade tumbling from the upper Etang de Joclar.

the Collada de Juclar on the Franco-Andorran frontier from where waymarks lead to the Col de l'Albe and a bouldery descent down to and around the Etangs de l'Albe and de Couart, the same route as described in the previous chapter, only in reverse. A few tents were squeezed into the few flat spots round the lake, most belonging, it seemed, to the anglers I could see sitting on boulders round the lake shores.

At the east end of the Etang de Couart, the path is left for a scrambly descent down a narrow ravine full of boulders that is the head of the Mourguillou valley. Once out of the ravine, a good path leads down by the stream to rejoin the start of the route near the Pont des Pierres. I stopped in the valley for lunch and checked my train timetables. There was a train to Toulouse in two hours. I did not have to catch it but for some reason I decided to try to do so, hastily shouldering my pack and dashing off down the valley. I was to be glad that I had made this decision for, as I reached the woods below the Pont des Pierres, the first thunder crashed overhead and the sky darkened. I rushed on downwards, almost running, to reach the station just as the downpour began. Fifteen minutes later I was sitting in the warmth of a railway carriage, gazing out at the torrential rain, my walk through the Haute Ariège already just a memory.

ROUTE

| Distance | | Place | Elevation | |
[km]	[miles]		[metres]	[feet]
0.0	0.0	Merens-les-Vals	1.050	3,444
10.0	6.0	Couillade de Llerbes	2,305	7,560
15.0	9.5	Refuge de Prat-Redon	1,809	5,934
17.0	10.5	Col de Beil	2,247	7,370
27.0	17.0	Refuge de Beille d'en Haut	1,939	6,360
33.0	20.5	Coudènes	1,040	3,411
42.0	26.0	Col du Sasc	1,798	5,897
49.0	30.5	Siguer	740	2,427
52.0	32.5	Lercoul pass	1,549	5,081
55.0	34.0	Col de Grail	1,485	4,871
59.0	36.5	Risoul pass	1,330	4,362
61.0	38.0	Goulier	1,110	3,641
65.0	40.5	Auzat	728	2,388
69.0	43.0	Arties	985	3,231
75.0	46.5	Etang d'Izourt	1,647	5,402
80.0	49.5	Refuge de l'Etang Fourcat	2,445	8,020
84.0	52.0	Gnioure stream	2,100	6,888
87.0	54.0	Pic d'Ariel	2,681	8,794
91.0	56.5	Etang de Soulanet	2,345	7,692
97.0	60.0	Col de l'Homme-Mort	2,526	8,285
102.0	63.5	Refuge de Garsan	1,895	6,216
107.0	66.5	Collada de Juclar	2,442	8,010
108.0	67.0	Col de l'Albe	2,539	8,328
114.0	71.0	Etang de Comte	1,726	5,661
119.0	74.0	Merens-les-Vals	1,050	3,444

From Merens-les-Vals, take the path leading up the wooded Mourgouillou valley. Soon after crossing the stone slabs of the Pont des Pierres, a junction is reached where the right-hand path, waymarked GR10, is taken up to and across the shoulder of the Pic de Savis and through downhill ski runs to the Couillade de Llerbes, from where a descending traverse leads to the Jasse des Llerbes. Reach the ridge to the west by a gentle climb, then descend steeply to the valley below and the Refuge de Prat-Redon. Now ascend the Ruisseau valley (no path) to the Col de Beil and turn north to traverse the rocky Crête des Isards before leaving the ridge to descend wide grassy slopes westwards to the Col de la Didorte.

An undulating walk over high pastureland takes you down to the Col des Finestres and then over Prat Moll to the Refuge de Beille d'en Haut, from where a complex descent (new bulldozed roads here) leads down through the Jasse d'Artaran and past the Clarans shelter to Coudènes and the Pont Orange. From the bridge, the path climbs up through the woods into the Calvière valley and then up the hillside to the Col de Sirmont and down again to the Sirbal valley. Climb out of this valley past the ruined Balledreyt shelter and then cross the hillside to the east of the Pic du Col Taillat to the Col du Sasc. Stay on the crest of the hills over Pla de Montcamp to the Col de Gamel and then descend through Gesties to the village of Siguer (bar but no supplies here). Next, climb steeply upwards to the village of Lercoul and then Lercoul pass, from where a path is followed through woods to the Col de Grail, then round the head of the Sem valley and down to Goulier and a field path to Auzat. A long ascent of the Arties valley on road and then footpath leads to the Etang d'Izourt.

Continuing south, the path climbs steeply to the Refuge l'Etang Fourcat and the start of a mostly pathless complex traverse of the mountains slopes north of the frontier. Cairns lead to the Etang de la Goueille and then the Gnioure stream. Difficult terrain has to be negotiated as the route crosses the ridge above near to the Etang de Rouch, descends into the Lassies cirques and then climbs to the summit of Pic d'Arial, from where the frontier ridge is followed over the Port de Siguer before you descend to the Etang de Soulanet and continue east over the Crête du Sal to the Col de l'Homme-Mort. From here there is a difficult crossing of the steep scree slopes above the Etang de Coume d'Ose before the Varilhes valley is descended to the Refuge de Garsan. Ascend south from the hut past the Etang de Joclar to the Collada de Juclar and a good path that leads over the Col de l'Albe and then down to the Etang de Couart. Here the path is left for a descent of the Mourgouillou valley past the Etang de Comte back to the Pont des Pierres and the path to Merens-les-Vals.

MAP

IGN Carte de Randonnées 1:50,000 No. 6 Andorre.

TRAIL GUIDES

Schwarz, Ros (translator/editor), *Walking the Pyrenees: GR10* (Robertson McCarta)
This translation of the French topo guide covers the route from the start to Etang d'Izourt and includes the maps for that section.

Veron, Georges, *Pyrenees High Level Route* (Gaston West Col)
Covers the section from Etang d'Izourt to Etang de Couart.

A Tour of the Carlit Massif:
L'Hospitalet to Merens-Les-Vals

> Solo wandering is often condemned, but no one may truly know the mountains till he has travelled alone among them the day long. Perceptions are keener, there is a fine sense of freedom, the idiosyncracies of one's companions need no longer be studied.
>
> **B.H. Humble**

East of the deep Ariège valley there lies one more high mountain wilderness before the Pyrenees fade slowly away into the Mediterranean. This is the Carlit massif, a compact but complex region of rugged granite peaks, narrow cliff-rimmed valleys and tarn-filled cirques; a final flourish of mountain glory before the descent into the rolling hills to the east. Although wholly in France, which elsewhere in the Pyrenees tends to mean cooler, wetter weather than south of the frontier, the Carlit is far enough east to have a hot, dry climate.

The almost circular shape of the area lends itself to a trek of that nature, with the railway line in the Ariège valley being the obvious place to start and finish. However, so as not to retrace too many steps, the route described here starts and finishes at different points on the railway line, namely the stations of L'Hospitalet and Merens-les-Vals. The walk could be done in either direction, the advantage of starting at L'Hospitalet being that it is 400 metres (1,312ft) higher than Merens-les-Vals. The walk is not particularly long but, as so often in the Pyrenees, length is not of great importance, the nature of the terrain having as much say in how far you go each day. Although much of the walking is on good paths, there are two mountain ascents involved which require the negotiation of steep

scree and rocks and a bit of route-finding. These could and perhaps should be avoided in bad weather. No mountaineering gear is needed, this being too far east and the peaks too low for there to be any permanent snowfields, but camping gear is essential as there are only a couple of staffed refuges and a few very basic shelters along the route. As always, though, the opportunities for marvellous wild camps are so great that it would be a crime to miss them.

The walk begins at L'Hospitalet railway station where I alighted from the Paris train into drizzle and low cloud – not a promising start. The start of the path, an HRP alternative route, will be found behind the Gendarmerie, from where it climbs steeply to a road above, which is followed to a hairpin bend. Here the path restarts, heading northwest above the Ariège valley out of which there rises the roar of traffic. Soon, though, the good hard-packed dirt trail curves west into the quieter confines of the Besines valley and the flower-filled gentle woods of the Bois Long. A surprise here is the appearance of an abandoned narrow-gauge railway track, presumably part of the workings for the building of the dam that lies ahead. The track leads to a solid flat-roofed refuge, the Refuge du Barage des Besines, which sleeps ten. As I passed, a figure stood outside chopping wood. A few

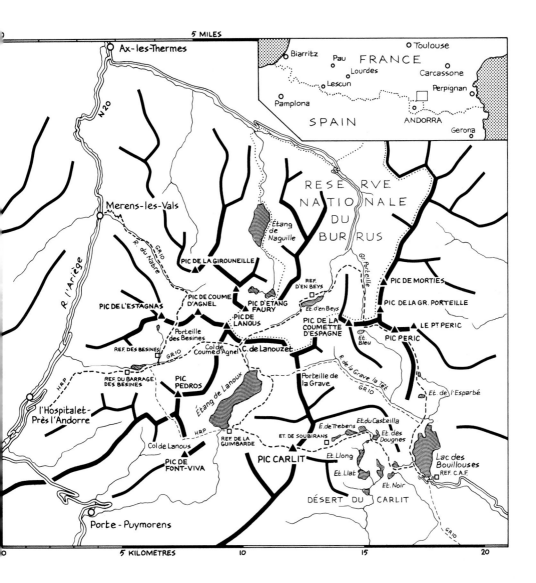

hundred metres more and the dam is reached and, beyond it, the waters of the reservoir. The path runs round the south side of this lake to some marshy pastureland at its head, across which can be seen the small Refuge des Besines which sleeps five. Smoke rising from the chimney showed that this, too, was occupied.

Opposite the refuge, the route joins the GR10 which comes in from the north. The path is waymarked with red and white paint blazes as it climbs beside the stream running into the reservoir to enter a large basin of woods, trickling streams, flower meadows and boulders; a lovely area with the 2,842m (9,322ft) pyramid of Pic Pedros rising above. I camped here, on one of many possible sites, on the banks of one of the streams. There

The author at a camp below Pic Pedros.

were two other tents pitched in this basin but it is so large that we were all out of sight of each other. Far too many fire rings dot the area, showing that this is a popular camping area. Unfortunately, these have been built on meadowland where fires should not be lit and no attempt has been made to dismantle them. However, it would be better to use one of these rings if you have a fire rather than risk damaging a new spot. Around the tent orchids were growing in the long grass, while across the stream black redstarts darted amongst the boulders. The evening was further enhanced as the weather started to brighten up, with patches of sunlight appearing through the clouds, though the cool breeze still had me wearing my fleece sweater, windshirt and hat as I wandered round the meadows.

Dawn came with a heavy dew and a clear sky. Above, Pic Pedros, the ascent of which looks feasible from here, glowed in the early sun, though it was 9 a.m. before its rays reached the tent. A Dipper bobbed on the rocks in the stream as I packed up for what turned out to be a longer, tougher and hotter day than I was expecting, the eventual near twenty kilometres (12½ miles) of distance and thousand metres (3,280ft) of ascent taking a good eight sweaty hours. Continuing up the GR10, the route leads into more rugged, steeper rocky terrain before levelling out at the Col de Coume d'Agnel. This is a major European watershed as the Besines stream to the west ends up in the Atlantic via the rivers Ariège and Garonne, while water from the Etang de Lanoux to the east runs to the Mediterranean by way of the rivers Carol, Sègre and Ebre. Of more immediate interest to

View west from the top of the descent from the north ridge of Pic Peric over the Petit Etang Bleu and the Etang Bleu to the Pic de la Coumette d'Espagne.

the walker is the superb views as the country ahead opens up. This is a surprise view, too, as the terrain is open and spacious, unlike the narrower, steeper-sided valley hemmed in with peaks that I had just ascended. Note particularly the highest rock pyramid on the horizon to the south-west. This is the Pic Carlit towards which we are headed.

From the col, I descended into the broad, grassy shallow cirque below and crossed wet meadows to pass the very small Etang de Lanouset and reach the northern shores of the very large Etang de Lanoux. There are plenty of places to camp here, though all of them are somewhat exposed to windy weather. As the path rounds the tip of the Lanoux lake, another trail joins it from the north. This is the GR7. In less than a kilometre the two long-distance paths split, the GR10 heading east to cross the Porteille de la Grave and then to descend to the Lac des Bouillouses; the GR7 turning south-west to traverse above the shores of the lake. Our route follows the latter path, though the GR10 would make a good bad-weather alternative as we, too, are heading for the Lac des Bouillouses, but by a longer and higher route.

The GR7 path stays some way above the waters of the lake, over which can be seen Pic Pedros, and then descends slightly to the tiny Refuge de la Guimbarde situated just above the dam at the southern end of the lake. The view of Pic Carlit from here is magnificent and the situation is, as Kev Reynolds says, idyllic. The vast amounts of garbage strewn in and around the hut rather detracted from this when I passed by, however, and I would not have liked to stay there. We join the HRP here, which comes in via the Col de Lanous from the Col de Puymorens to the west, a shorter alternative start to the route.

The ascent of Pic Carlit, a steep, narrow rocky ridge of a peak, starts at the refuge on a good path that leads up the Fourats valley to the Etang de Fourats. The mountain looks imposing, not to say dauntingly steep and rocky, from here. Note the Y-shaped scree gully just to the north of the summit. The path, visible as a pale winding line from the lake, goes up this, taking the right-hand branch where the gully splits, a long hard scree slog, especially with a heavy pack on a hot day, but nowhere difficult. The small neat summit, at 2,921m (9,581ft) the highest in the eastern Pyrenees, is just a brief walk south of the col at the top of the gully. The views are extensive as there are no other high peaks nearby. Distant forests, green valleys and rolling hills are visible to the south and east, with higher, more rugged mountains to the north and west, but these were lapped by clouds when I was there. Closer to hand, though far below, lie deep, rocky cirques and a series of upland tarns. Steep slopes fall away abruptly from the peak to these, leaving you in no doubt that you are on a mountain top. I shared the view with two other walkers who nearly lost their map, spread out to aid them in identifying distant features, in the gusty wind that had me donning my windshirt.

The descent to the east is not quite as

Meren-les-Vals railway station.

Walkers on the start of the ascent of Pic Carlit.

simple as described in the trail guides, though it is the most popular ascent route with day walkers as the round trip can easily be done in a day from the roadhead at the Lac des Bouillouses. I could see many people descending and a few ascending from the col to the north of the summit, to which you return before dropping a short way down the scree to the east. Do not continue into the narrowing gully below, however, as there are crags there but traverse towards the right on to a steep rocky buttress. The path, marked by cairns and boot-smoothed and whitened granite, weaves a sometimes exposed way across through the rocks and descends a number of short but narrow and steep chimneys where hands are required and which are awkward with a large pack. This route is certainly harder than the one from the Lanoux lake.

Throughout, though, there are good views of the necklace of lakes leading through the wide, verdant valley below, by one of which I intended to camp.

Eventually, the route down the buttress becomes easier and then starts to level off as the first lake is approached. The path splits here, the main branch heading east to the Etangs Balleil, Long, Lat, Coumasse and Sec to be rejoined by the alternative at the Etang du Vive. Seeking a camp site, I took the latter path passing by the Etangs Soubirans, Trebens and Casteilla to camp near the Etang des Dougnes. I would have stopped by Trebens where the sites look superb but there were already tents here and the noise of the occupants' radio was so loud that I could hear it long before I reached the lake and long afterwards, too, which also ruled out a camp by Casteilla. That evening the view was superb across the wind-rippled waters of the small lake to distant hills away to the south-east lit palely by the fading sun. So it was the next morning when the waters were calm, the wind (which had reached its peak with powerful gusts that shook the tent, waking me in the process, at 1.30 a.m.) having died away with the dawn.

By 8.30 a.m. the sun was already high in the sky and the first day-walkers were on the move. Another very hot and, for me, long and tough day was beginning. Initially, though, the descent on a well-used path past more lakes and into woods that leads to the Lac des Bouillouses is pleasant and easy. The highlight of this short section is the view over the blue waters of the Etang du Vive to the distant grey-brown isolated peak of Pic Peric, where we are headed. Many people passed me heading up and my 'bonjours' became well practised. Two parties asked me the way to Pic Carlit. Follow the path and the other people, I replied. At the Lacs des Bouillouses there is a sudden eruption of cars, people and noise.

Across the dam lies the staffed Combaleran refuge for those seeking accommodation, though apparently this is usually full during the height of the summer season. If you are not staying here, the noise and bustle, but not all the people, are quickly left behind as the GR10 is taken north through the woods on the west side of the lake. At the far end, the wide grassy Tet valley is reached where there are many fine places to pitch a tent. The GR10 turns north-west up this valley for the Porteille de la Grave, this being the point at which those who have crossed that pass rather than ascend Pic Carlit rejoin the main route.

The Tet stream is crossed by a shaky wooden bridge, then a winding path is taken north through tree groves and up open hillsides with good views of the peak ahead until the Etang de l'Esparbe can be seen to the right. Here, leave the path and aim directly for the base of the south ridge of Pic Peric, an easy walk through continuing parkland-like scenery. As the path continues up the Llose valley to the Grande Porteille d'Espagne where we are also headed, it would seem to provide

Drinking water in Merens-les-Vals.

an alternative route. However, if the weather makes climbing Pic Peric unwise, then attempting the descent into the Grande Porteille cirque is even less advisable.

The terrain changes abruptly when the ridge is reached, a very steep grass and rock climb being needed to surmount its steep buttress-like termination. The ridge proper is then quite easy to climb, though very stony, until a section of loose, shattered pinnacles is reached. These proved too difficult and exposed to scramble over with a heavy pack, at least for me, so I backtracked a little, then descended steep scree and turned on their east side, contouring across to the east ridge where a good path leads easily to the summit. I noted that a couple behind me on the ridge turned back before I did and that there was little sign of a path. The standard ascent appears to come up the Puig valley east of the south ridge to the col between the main peak and the Petit Peric. This could be easily reached by contouring north-east round the base of the ridge.

The views from the tiny neat 2,810m (9,217ft) summit, which I had to myself though I could see people on the Petit Peric, are good and all-embracing, with the tangled rugged mountains of the high Pyrenees disappearing into the west, a great contrast to the gentle pastoral woods and vales and green hills that roll into the east. Northwards, however, clouds were rolling in. So, after twenty minutes, I cut short my stay and descended the north ridge a few metres until a steep scree gully appeared on the left. I descended this until I could contour round under the north ridge to a col on the ridge that runs between the Pic de la Coumette d'Espange and the Pic de la Grande Porteille. Below this col to the south lies the Petit Etang Bleu, by which a camp could be made. To the north lies an intimidatingly steep descent. Initially, this lies down one of several gullies. Whichever one

you choose (they all look horrendous), take great care as there are crags and steep slabs below.

Once out of the gully on to more open slopes you can breathe a little more easily, the descent now merely being on nasty, steep loose scree and boulders. This leads into a desolate rocky basin in which lie the cold pools of the Etangs de la Grande Porteille. Over on the gentler western slopes of this basin a path can be seen descending, mostly on grass. Where this begins I do not know but it must come down from somewhere on the ridge above and it could be worth continuing west from the col above the Petit Etang Bleu in the hope of locating it or at the least a safer and easier way down that leads to it. The map, in fact, does show the route as descending from the Grande Porteille d'Estagne above the west end of the Etang Bleu and almost a kilometre along the ridge from the col above the Petit Etang Bleu. This descent is the same as that given by Kev Reynolds in *Walks and Climbs in the Pyrenees* and I have seen no written description of the one marked on the map.

Throughout the difficult first part of this descent I was uncomfortably aware that I was alone in an area that looked little visited and that no one knew exactly where I was. If anything happened – and this was terrain where I felt an accident could all too easily occur – it would be ten days or more before anyone back in Britain began to wonder why I had not returned. These thoughts made me take great care as I descended, though at the same time I tried to go as fast as I could as the clouds to the north were approaching rapidly and I did not want to be caught up there in a storm. The thought of negotiating this terrain when wet and slippery as well as in thick mist filled me with horror. The concentration required for a safe descent made me aware I was quite tired, too, and I began to wish I had camped at the Petit Etang Bleu and left these

View south over the Etang des Dougnes

difficulties until the morning.

Once past the lakes where there was no ground I could see that would hold a tent peg, all being bare rock, I picked up a faint path and some occasional cairns. When grass appeared I considered camping, but the stream bed here was dry and the water in the few tiny pools nearby looked murky and unappetizing. As I had no idea how far I might have to go to find purer water if I stopped, and as the mist was closing in all around while thunder began to rumble overhead, I pushed on, despite increasing tiredness and sore legs and feet. The descent continues down a dry, scree-filled ravine that is just steep and rocky enough to make progress slow and difficult ('uncomfort-able' is Reynolds' description). I slithered down the stones, thankful I had a staff to help me keep on my feet, until near the bottom I

was able to abandon the ravine for the thickly vegetated slopes to the side. Finally, the terrain levelled out just before a small hydro-electric plant.

I stopped at the first piece of flat ground and made camp close to where a refreshing stream ran. I had barely finished pitching the tent when two walkers approached out of the mist want-ing to know where they were. As they were Italians and spoke no English and I speak no Italian, we had to converse in broken French that was equally bad on both sides. Luckily I could show them on the map where we were which had them heading back down the valley looking, as far as I could gather, for the Refuge d'En Beys which lay four kilometres (2½ miles) away in the main valley below. Once they had gone, I lit my little gas stove and had a couple of mugs of coffee followed by some soup and a quick-cook pasta meal flavoured with garlic and extra cheese. By the time I had finished this lengthy supper I felt relaxed again, the tensions of the descent having eased away. Outside, the mist drifted in and out of the trees just visible on the ridge opposite the tent. The thunder had amounted to nothing and all was calm when I drifted off to sleep.

The tent was wet with dew at dawn and the mist had gone, though clouds filled the sky and covered the peaks. These soon cleared, too, and I slid out of my sleeping bag and the tent to see where I had pitched. I found myself in a narrow valley hemmed in by high walls which I was admiring when I glimpsed movement. A dozen isards were running quickly across the hillside a short way down the valley. Seeing them made for a good start

to the day as did the discovery of a clear path leading round the steep bluff to the west that gave excellent views into the deep Oriège valley to the north. This path contours into the upper reaches of this valley to join the GR7 which comes up the valley bottom shortly before the Etang d'En Beys is reached. On the north shore of this lake sits the staffed CAF Refuge d'En Beys that the two Italians had been seeking. Many people were sitting outside it and there were several tents pitched at the head of the lake as I passed; I felt I had returned to a land containing other walkers and climbers left, if only briefly, when I had descended from the summit of Pic Peric. Beyond the lake the path winds through a beautiful narrow valley rich with brilliant-coloured flowers and many darting lizards. At one point I saw an adder sliding through the

The author on the top of Pic Peric.

grass. It was an idyllic place but also very, very hot as the enclosing granite walls reflected back the sun and held in the totally still, burning air.

At a lovely tarn high in the valley I stopped for a rest and to admire the massive granite boulders, one of which I used as a backrest, and which make up most of the terrain here. The path hereabouts is sketchy but at some point it is meant to divide. Failing to locate this junction, I simply headed straight up the back of the cirque to emerge on to the wide ridge above, a kilometre or so east of the Col de Coume d'Agnel which I reached by an easy contour, relishing the cool breeze that blew across the open slopes. It is possible to continue up the ridge to the Pic de Lanous before crossing to the col if you want to bag a quick peak. At the col the ascent route is reversed all the way down to the Refuge des Besines. Here, though, we turn north-east for the easy climb to the Porteille des Besines

where marmots may be seen darting about in the rocks. The final descent of the walk starts here on a rocky track through boulder fields. Looking back, the amazing black fang of rock at the end of the south-east ridge of the Pic de l'Estagnas can be seen rearing into the sky and dominating the view. Just below the bright algae green l'Estagnas tarn and before the steep drop into the Nabre valley, I stopped and made camp on somewhat lumpy ground in the trees by the stream. To the north could be seen the serrated crest of the Pic de Girouneille while above to the east rose the Pic de Coume d'Agnel. It was a fine site.

At 6.30 a.m. it was calm and clear, though there was no sign of the sun even on the peaks. A dew lay on the tent and the temperature was 8°C (46°F). At 7.15 the first rays of the sun touched the summits above, but the valley was still deep in shadow and was cool as I descended to the Nabre stream and then down its long valley. Lower down, the

Cow with cow bell.

Walkers descending the gully on Pic Carlit to the Etang des Fourats.

path was lined with delicious ripe raspberries and tangled woods of hazel, birch, oak and rowan. Ruined farm buildings appear and then the path reaches Merens-d'en-Haut and passes a picturesque ruined Romanesque church. GR10 waymarks lead the final few hundred metres past a gites d'étape, over the Nabre river and into Merens-les-Vals where I was soon sitting at a shady restaurant table celebrating my successful Tour of the Carlit with an excellent meal.

ROUTE

Distance		Place	Elevation	
[km]	[miles]		[metres]	[feet]
0.0	0.0	L'Hospitalet	1,436	4,710
7.0	4.5	Refuge des Besines	1,981	6,498
10.0	6.0	Col de Coume d'Agnel	2,470	8,102
17.0	10.5	Refuge de la Guimbarde	2,250	7,380
21.0	13.0	Pic Carlit	2,921	9,581
28.0	17.5	Lac des Bouillouses	2,020	6,626
31.0	19.5	Tet valley	2,000	6,560
36.0	22.5	Pic Peric	2,810	9,217
43.0	26.5	Etang d'En Beys	1,954	6,409
48.0	30.0	Porteille d'Orlu	2,475	8,131
52.0	32.5	Refuge des Besines	1,981	6,498
54.0	33.5	Porteille des Besines	2,320	7,610
61.0	38.0	Merens-les-Vals	1,050	3,444

From L'Hospitalet, take the path north-west to a road which is followed to a hairpin bend where it is left for a wide track leading round the hillside and into the Besines valley. Pass the Besines lake and the Refuge des Besines to pick up GR10 waymarks which lead on up the valley to the Col de Coume d'Agnel. Descend wide slopes, still on the GR10, to the head of the Etang de Lanoux where the GR10 is left for the path running south-west above the lake to the tiny Refuge de la Guimbarde. Turn south-east here to ascend the Fourats valley to the Etang des Fourats and then the steep scree gully and final rocks to the summit of Pic Carlit. Drop down the gully to the east a short way, then cut across the rocky slopes to the south on a rough path to descend a broad buttress to the series of lakes that leads to the Desert du Carlit and then the large reservoir of the Lac des Bouillouses, where there is a hotel and a CAF refuge.

Head north now along the wooded banks of the lake to the grassy Tet valley. Cross the stream by a rickety bridge and then take the path past the Etang de l'Esparde to the foot of the south ridge of Pic Peric. The ridge can be scrambled along but the easiest route up this peak is by the col between it and le Petit Peric, reached via the valley east of the south ridge. From the summit of Pic Peric, descend the north ridge a short way and then go west down a scree gully to contour to a col north of the Petit Etang Bleu. Here, either carefully descend scree to the Etang de la Grande Porteille or follow the ridge west to the Grande Porteille d'Espagne and descend from there. Once safely in the bowl below, descend beside the stream and then via a good path round the hillside to the west to the Etang d'En Beys and the Refuge d'En Beys. Continue up the valley past the Etang Faury to the ridge at its head from where you can contour to the Col de Coume d'Agnel and descend the ascent route to the Refuge des Besines. An easy climb on the GR10 leads north to the Porteille des Besines and then down to the Nabre valley and Merens-les-Vals.

MAP

IGN Carte de Randonnées 1:50,000 No. 8 Cerdagne-Capcir.

TRAIL GUIDES

Reynolds, Kev, *Walks and Climbs in the Pyrenees* (Cicerone Press)
Schwarz, Ros (translator/editor), *Walking the Pyrenees: GR10* (Robertson McCarta)
Veron, Georges, *Pyrenees High Level Route* (Gaston West Col)

Between all three the whole route is covered.

The Long Walks:
From the Atlantic to the Mediterranean

> For my part, I travel not to go anywhere but to go. I travel for travel's sake. The great affair is to move; to feel the needs and hitches of our lives more nearly; to come down off this feather-bed of civilisation, and find the globe granite underfoot and strewn with cutting flints.
>
> Robert Louis Stevenson
> **Travels with a Donkey**

A linear mountain range like the Pyrenees, especially one that stretches from sea to sea, invites, indeed challenges, the walker to traverse it from one end to the other. Such a venture was, as far as is known, first successfully undertaken as long ago as 1817 when Dr Frederic Parrot of Estonia walked from the Atlantic to the Mediterranean in fifty-three days, stopping off along the way to make first ascents of a number of mountains, most notably 3,308m (10,850ft) Pico de la Maladetta. Since then, two very different routes have been worked out along the full length of the range, the Grande Randonnée 10 and the Haute Randonnée Pyrénéene.

As the Pyrenees are over 400 kilometres (248 miles) in length, any end-to-end walk is obviously a major undertaking and one that will probably take the best part of a summer. Those who are familiar with the logistics of long-distance walking will know that any route will invariably be at least 50 per cent longer than the straight-line distance between its beginning and end. This holds true for the Pyrenees, with the GR10 being around 700 kilometres (435 miles) long and the HRP, a more difficult route to measure because of all the variations, at least 600 kilometres (373 miles). Because of the rugged nature of the terrain and the huge amount of ascent involved on each route, even the strongest

walker will do well to average 20–25 kilometres (12½–15½ miles) a day and most are likely to settle for 12–15 kilometres (7½–9½ miles). This means that somewhere between thirty and sixty days would be required for either walk. Looked at in these terms, Dr Parrot's fifty-three days is a very fast time for an age before footpaths, waymarks and mountain refuges; before, in fact, the range had even been fully explored.

Neither of the two standard trail guides, that is the GR10 topo guide (translated as *Walking the Pyrenees*) and Georges Verons's *Pyrenees High Level Route*, gives distances. Instead, they use the time an 'average' walker might take to measure the route, a practice I find irritating as different people walk at very different rates and I for one do not want to finish every day at the same place everyone else does. The topo guide, without saying what walking speed is the basis for the calculations, gives times in hours and minutes, not days, and there is no running total. However, added together, the figure is around 350 hours which would mean that if you walked for seven hours a day (rest stops not included) the walk would take fifty days. In contrast, the HRP guide is divided into forty-five day stages, though times for shorter sections as well as each stage are included in the text. These times are based on 4.5

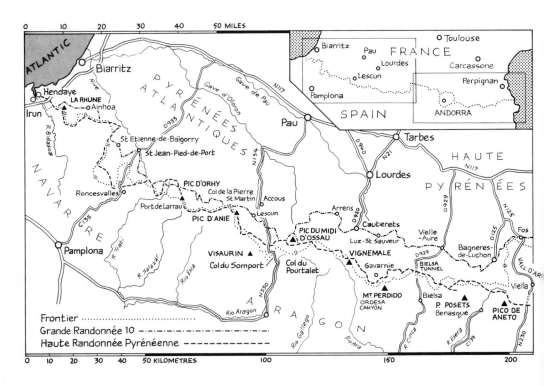

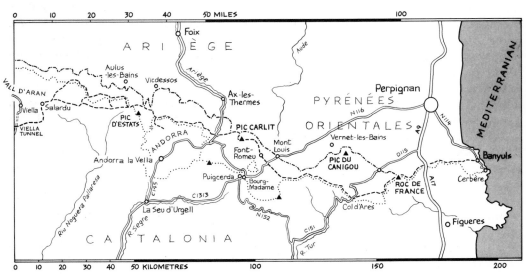

kilometres (2¾ miles) per hour on the flat and 350 metres (1,148ft) of ascent per hour and Veron does warn that 'each trekker will have to interpret these times according to his/her own performance'.

The one person I have met actually engaged in a full traverse was combining sections of the GR10 and HRP and had been walking for thirty-four days when I met him in the Haute Ariège. He was reckoning on taking another fourteen days to finish, making a total of forty-eight days. At the time of writing, I am tentatively planning a double traverse, heading east along the GR10 and then returning west along the HRP, for which my estimated time is seventy to eighty days. And the conclusion to all this? You need to have six or more weeks to spare if you want to walk one of these routes in its entirety and enjoy it.

While the two routes often touch and occasionally run together, they are very different in character, the GR10 being wholly in France and, in theory at least, all on good, waymarked paths (the GR blaze consists of two painted lines, one red, one white). In practice, this is not always so, however; *see* the chapter, 'A Tour of the Haute Ariège' for a description of the route-finding difficulties I encountered when walking that section. Although it ventures high into the mountains in places, the GR10 never crosses difficult terrain or enters into the realm of the mountaineer. Instead, this is a route of wooded valleys, rich meadows and picturesque villages as well as mountain tarns and passes, a low-level route for the lover of mountain and forest scenery who does not want to explore the heights or spend days high above timberline and who prefers to walk mostly on clear footpaths and dine frequently on good food in pleasant restaurants rather than on the dried rations of the wilderness backpacker. This is also the route for those who prefer blankets to sleeping bags, and beds to the hard ground, as there is plenty of accommodation along the way, too, ranging from tiny mountain refuges to gites d'étapes to small hotels. Heavy packs are not needed either, as your tent can be left at home and mountaineering gear such as ice axe and crampons are unnecessary. However, it would be wise to carry a sleeping bag, a small stove with a little fuel and some food for those nights, few in number, but unavoidable unless you are prepared and able to walk very long distances on some days, where your shelter will be a small shepherd's cabin or hut in which the only facilities will be the roof and four walls and perhaps a bunk.

The HRP, however, as the name suggests, stays as close to the crest of the range as is practicable, often crossing steep, pathless terrain, where route-finding skills and scrambling ability are required, and ascending several peaks. While it stays north of the frontier for much of the way, the HRP does dip into Spain on occasion, sometimes for considerable distances. Sections may be cairned and there are frequent paths, but there are no HRP waymarks as such. Although there are many huts along the route, especially in the Parc National des Pyrénées, there are also long sections where a tent is required, making it a trek for the experienced mountain backpacker prepared and used to carrying a heavy load. No concessions are made for resupplying either, a week or more's food needing to be carried for certain sections unless long diversions are made. Also, unlike the GR10, the HRP is not a set route, there being a multitude of variations, with three or four options running in parallel in some areas. Indeed, the sub-title of Georges Veron's guide to the route is 'Mountain Walking and Trekking Guide for a Complete Traverse of the Range in 45 Day Stages with 50 Easier or Harder Alternatives and Variations'. In other words, the optional stages outnumber the 'official' ones! This really makes the HRP an idea, a vision even, around which you can construct your own route, rather than a fixed line which is to be followed religiously. Few people who have walked the HRP will have trodden exactly the same routes.

These long paths are so important that it is worth looking at each one in detail, even though most walkers visiting the Pyrenees will not have the time to do either one in its entirely in one trek, which is why I have left the description of them until the last chapter. Many sections of both routes have already been described as it is impossible to walk far in the Pyrenees without coming across them. In fact, it may well be that their greatest value is in providing ideas for the shorter one- or two-week treks that are the norm. Although I have spent enough days along sections of both the GR10 and the HRP to feel I have an understanding of the individual characteristics each one has, I have not done either of them from one end to the other. It is nice to have some ambitions left!

THE GRANDE RANDONNÉE 10: Sentier des Pyrénées

Over 40,000 kilometres (24,840 miles) of footpaths make up France's Grande Randonnée network. The body responsible for creating, maintaining and waymarking this system of routes has the rather unwieldly if grand title of La Federation Française de Randonnée Pedestre, Comité National des Sentiers de Grande Randonnée. All the paths have numbers, hence GR10, the path of the Pyrenees.

Starting on the coast of the Atlantic Ocean in the west, as it is advisable to do, so that the prevailing weather will be at your back, at the little seaside resort of Hendaye-Plage, the GR10 first meanders through the wooded hills and well-watered, verdant sheep pastures, thick with gorse and bracken, of the Basque country, passing through many pretty villages and never reaching even 2,000 metres (6,560ft) in height. After 180 or so kilometres (112 miles), though, the scenery changes as the karst limestone country around the Pic d'Anie is reached and the path enters the High Pyrenees. The light feel of limestone scenery with its white rocks and bright green pastures is kept as the path crosses the Aspe valley and passes the distinctive peak of the Pic du Midi d'Ossau, around which there is an optional but recommended circular walk.

Beyond the Pic du Midi, granite becomes the dominant rock, and the terrain of the high mountains becomes more rugged, too rugged for the GR10 which heads north into the gentler foothills; once past the grim fastnesses of the Balaitous, there is another recommended *variante* that runs south from the spa town of Cauterets to pass under the impressive north face of the Vingemale and then descend to Gavarnie, from where the famous cirque can be visited. This option then heads north down the Gave valley to rejoin the main route at Luz St-Sauveur. From there, the Neouvielle massif, a wilderness of lakes and desolate granite peaks and an important nature reserve standing alone well north of the frontier, is crossed to the Vallée d'Aure, from where the frontier is paralleled to Bagnères-de-Luchon situated just about half-way along the range.

Staying resolutely in France, the GR10 is forced north next in order to avoid the anomaly of the Vall d'Aran which, although north of the watershed, is in Spain. Much of the way here is in woodland, as the route continues well north of the Andorran frontier to skirt the edges of the Haute Ariège. Here, the undulating path crosses the ends of the many spurs that extend north from the high mountains so there is much steep ascent and descent but also good views and excellent

Refuge du Barrage des Besines.

scenery. The Ariège river itself is crossed at Meren-les-Vals, beyond which the GR10 ventures for the last time into the higher mountains with a crossing of the sparkling lake-strewn terrain of the Carlit massif. Beyond this lies the Cerdagne and then a low pleasant decline into the hot dusty hills bordering the Mediterranean, the route finishing in the seaside resort of Banyuls-sur-Mer.

THE HAUTE RANDONNÉE PYRÉNÉENE

While the GR10 is a scenic route and one well worth walking, it does skirt most of the highest, most rugged and most impressive parts of the Pyrenees, the very regions that adventurous trekkers will want to seek out. For them the Haute Randonnée Pyrénéene (High Level Route), a creation of the French Alpine Club (CAF), is ideal, a rugged mountain traverse requiring scrambling, route-finding and camping skills and the ability to cope with remote, difficult and, in places, snow-covered terrain. Hour after hour, day after day, week after week, the spectacular scenery unfolds with high peaks, glaciers and snowfields, deep lake-filled cliff-rimmed cirques and rushing mountain torrents abounding. There is much wildlife, too, with isards and marmots common, while in the air vultures and eagles can often be seen soaring. For the botanist, the mixture of Mediterranean and alpine plant life makes the region unique. Is anything missed out of this marvellous walk? Well, yes, the Ordesa Canyon, a feature peculiar only to the Pyrenees and one that I would include in any end-to-end walk, probably by the route described in the chapter, 'A Tour of Gavarnie'.

The route begins quietly enough, as it has to, there being no high mountains in the misty, wooded Basque country at the western end of the range, sharing its starting point, Hendaye-Plage, and the first few kilometres with the GR10. Unlike that route, though, for much of the way through this region the HRP follows the pathless crest of the hills, often running along the frontier itself and occasionally wandering into Spain. I have not walked in this area but the trail guide warns that mists are frequent, making navigation quite difficult in the often featureless rolling terrain, where the only paths may be those made by the myriad sheep.

As with the GR10, the whole nature of the route changes when the spectacular karst limestone scenery is reached around Pic d'Anie and the wonderful Cirque d'Ansabère, the start of the real mountains. From here, the HRP drops into Spain then climbs back up to a high pass, and entry into the Parc National des Pyrénées, to wind in and out of the frontier summits along high mountain paths, past remote lonely tarns and jagged cliffs. To the south, the dusty, faded sierras of Spain dissolve into the hazy horizon and to the north the dark-green wooded valleys of France sink into the distance. Ahead across the deep wooded confines of the Aspe valley, the towering block of pale limestone that is the Pic du Midi d'Ossau draws the walker on until you are walking beneath its massive cliffs marvelling at the glory all around.

Beyond the Pic du Midi, a grimmer, more savage landscape is entered; the harsh granite land of the Balaitous, the most westerly of the 3,000m (9,840ft) summits. This is difficult country to traverse and the first of the major alternative routes is offered here. The main route crosses the massif to the north of the frontier over several high passes and across steep, difficult and remote terrain – a trek for good weather and the experienced mountain walker. The easier alternative drops south into Spain to follow a softer, greener valley before returning to France by the Col de la Fache and joining the main route in the lovely Marcadau valley.

As so often, the route next heads straight back up into the mountains to cross below the great north face of the Vingemale with its cracked and broken glaciers and then curves round to traverse high slopes on the very walls of the Cirque de Gavarnie. The HRP itself avoids the actual village of Gavarnie but few walkers will, this being the first supply point near the route since Lescun below the Cirque d'Ansabère at the start of the High Pyrenees. Scorning the softness of the town, the HRP

Gite d'Etape sign.

Burnt-out Romanesque church in Merens-d'en-Haut.

dips and soars over high pass after high pass as it takes the walker on a tour of the great cirques abutting the frontier east of Gavarnie: Estaube, Troumouse and Barroude and then on below the frontier to the Hospice de Rioumajou, from where it climbs to a pass and enters Spain again.

Here, another choice presents itself as the main route returns to France with another trek across tarn-filled rocky cirques below the frontier, while the alternative crosses the Puerto de Gistain and descends the beautiful tree-dotted Valle de Estos below the Posets massif to its junction with the Esera valley. This is then followed, sadly on a road, into the rugged country of the Maladetta and below the Pico de Aneto, the highest mountain

in the Pyrenees. As the main route cuts back over from France to join the alternative one in the upper Esera valley, the latter would seem the most logical itinerary. Whichever option is chosen, there next comes the highest part of the route, the crossing of the jagged, narrow and steep-sided 2,900m (9,512ft) Mullères ridge, an arduous climb in a bleak rock landscape involving an element of scrambling and requiring careful route-finding, especially in bad weather. Note that the descent is just as difficult as the ascent and very long, it being 1,300m (4,264ft) down to the Hospice de Viella.

The route stays in Spain for a while to cross the lovely magic country of the Encantados before heading north to the frontier and a wealth of route choices. The Haute Ariège in France is a wild, rugged area that until recently was little visited. It still has few paths and few huts and any traverse of it requires confidence and experience. When the HRP was first developed the easier southern side was chosen for this section, the main route passing through long Spanish valleys well south of the frontier and then crossing through the northern reaches of Andorra. Now, however, there is an alternative HRP on the French side plus a spider's web of routes connecting the two and offering other options. In places, three routes run in parallel. The walks either side of the frontier are both superb and I, and I am sure many others, would find it impossible to choose between them. Only in bad weather would the decision be at all easy, as then the easier southern option, where there are paths and the terrain is less rugged and runs well below the peaks, would be by far the safest and most pleasant route. Also, the likelihood is that the conditions would be far better there as well.

Beyond the Haute Ariège the route, alternatives and all, returns wholly to France for a crossing of the last high mountain massif before the sea, the marvellous tarn-dotted granite wilderness of the Carlit. Not, however, that the walk is over once you are through, as you are all too quickly, this superb region. There remains the crossing of the wide, green meadows of the Cerdagne and then a ridge-top rolling walk that includes the ascent of the last high peak on the route, 2,784m (9,132ft) Pic Canigou, followed by a final gentle descent along the same route as the GR10 to Banyuls-sur-Mer.

MAPS

For the HRP: Carte de Randonnées Pyrenees 1:50,000 Nos. 1–9, plus Editorial Alpina 1:25,000: Posets, Maladetta-Aneto; 1:40,000: Vall d'Aran, Pica d'Estats-Mont Roig.

TRAIL GUIDES

Castle, Alan *Across the Pyrenees: the GR10* (Cicerone Press)
Schwarz, Roz (translator/editor) *Walking the Pyrenees: GR10* (Robertson McCarta)
This translation of the French topo guide covers the whole route and contains sections of all the 1:50,000 maps.
Veron, Georges *Pyrenees High Level Route* (Gaston West Col)

Practical Considerations

> *I fastened a hard, durable crust to my belt by way of provision, in case I should be compelled to pass a night on the mountain-top.*
>
> John Muir

GENERAL LOGISTICS

The Pyrenees are easily accessible by rail or road. Although a car provides the freedom to move relatively quickly from area to area, it has big disadvantages. Many of the routes, both those described in this book and other obvious ones are linear, which leaves car-borne walkers with the problem of how to return to their vehicles. Also, two days would be needed for the drive to the Pyrenees, while the train journey takes little more than twenty-four hours. The overall costs are probably about the same. If a sleeping compartment is booked from Paris you can arrive feeling fresh and relaxed and able to start walking within minutes of stepping off the train. Many of the routes start and finish at railway stations and those that do not can be quickly reached from them by local buses or taxis. For linear routes, it is possible to book via a central point such as Toulouse or Lourdes on to branch lines to the start and from the finish of the walk. For these reasons, I have always travelled to the Pyrenees by train. Up-to-date information on train times and fares can be obtained from:

The European Rail Travel Centre,
Victoria Station,
London SW1.
Tel: 071-834 2345

Food can be bought in all towns and most of the larger villages but smaller places may not have shops, so it is wise to assume that they will not and treat any that appear as a bonus. Even where there are several stores, the choice may not be very great. Anyone who can find breakfast cereals is doing better than me! If you resupply as you go along, expect to live on bread, crackers, cheese, packet soups, tinned goods and chocolate and granola bars, not in itself a bad diet for the mountains. Users of staffed huts will, of course, eat there. Only on one of the routes, that described in the first chapter, is it necessary to carry food for any length of time (7–10 days), though, of course, side trips and ascents will add days on to the time spent in the mountains on other walks.

Most places, even those without shops, have restaurants and I have found the food invariably excellent. Indeed, one the pleasures of walking in the Pyrenees is to dine out, after days spent on dehydrated rations, at a tiny hotel-restaurant at a remote valley-head with the peaks towering overhead. I now always include such stops in my planning.

RESCUE AND INSURANCE

Although the likelihood of an accident happening to a walker is remote, the possibility must be considered. On the French side there is an efficient, professional but expensive rescue service. On the Spanish side you will have to rely on voluntary help. In either case, the costs can be great so some form of insurance is essential. Schemes for mountain walkers and trekkers are offered by the following two bodies, amongst others:

BMC Services Ltd.,
Insurance Department,
Crawford House,
Precinct Centre,
Booth Street East,
Manchester M13 9RZ.
Tel: 061–273 5163

West Mercia Insurance Services,
High Street,
Wombourne,
Nr Wolverhampton WV5 9DN.
Tel: 0902 892661

TOURIST INFORMATION

For general information, such as details of accommodation in the main centres, contact:

French Government Tourist Office,
178 Piccadilly,
London W1V 0AL.
Tel: 071–493 6594

Spanish National Tourist Office,
57 St James's Street,
London SW1A 1LD.
Tel: 071–499 0901

ACCESS AND CAMPING

There is no restriction to walking anywhere in most of the Pyrenees, though footpaths should be adhered to when crossing farmland, but there are limitations on where you can camp in some protected regions. In the Pyrenees National Park camping is only allowed an hour or more's walk from the nearest road, while in the Ordesa National Park it is only allowed above the 2,000m (6,560ft) contour line, which means not in the canyon itself. Also, camping is forbidden or limited to certain areas around some of the larger staffed huts in the PNP, not places the lover of solitude or pristine wilderness would want to camp anyway. In the Neouvielle Nature Reserve, camping is forbidden except on areas set aside for this purpose (and looking very worn on account of that) near the Chalet-Hôtel d'Oredon and at the southern end of Lac d'Aubert. In the lower valleys there are many organized sites as there are in most of the popular tourist towns and villages like Luchon and Gavarnie.

Mountain flowers.

HUTS

There are three types of refuge for walkers found in the Pyrenees: basic unlocked shelters, staffed mountain huts and gites d'étape. The first are usually small, often single-roomed, and generally provide nothing but a roof over your head and perhaps bunks to sleep on. They are useful as alternatives to tents in bad weather but can become overcrowded, hot and stuffy. I have more than once abandoned trying to sleep in one and dragged my sleeping bag outside to bivvy under the stars or even in the rain.

Staffed mountain huts provide meals and bedding, so using them means you can carry a much lighter load than if you camp. The penalties, however, are that you have to plan your walks so as to reach one each evening and they can be noisy and crowded. My extremely limited experience of them has put me off so much that I no longer consider using them.

However, if you are going to do so they are cheaper if you are a member of the Club Alpin Français, who run many of them. The CAF can also provide a list of huts. The address is:

Club Alpin Français,
7 rue la Boetie,
Paris 75008,
France.

Gites d'étape are found mostly in the valleys and provide mattresses, cooking facilities and, in many cases, meals. They are run by the following organization who again can provide a list of them:

Randonnées Pyrénéenes,
3 Place Balague,
090200 St-Girons,
France.

SEASONS/WEATHER

The Pyrenees are a southern range and the climate reflects that of the Mediterranean. This is especially so on the Spanish side which is generally hotter and drier than the French one (hint: if you are getting drenched in France, cross the border!). I have often stood on the frontier ridge with cloud-filled French valleys on one side and dusty Spanish ones, shimmering in a heat haze, on the other. This contrast means that a clash of hot dry air coming up from the south and cool wet air from the north occurs over the frontier, a mix that produces thunderstorms seemingly out of nowhere, usually in the late afternoon. For this reason, it is wise to be down from any high point soon after midday. The summer season starts in mid-June, though a fair amount of snow may still remain then on the higher slopes, and crevasses will be covered. From then until late September marks the period for high-level walking. Generally, the weather is dry, though depressions bringing rain may last for a few days at a time, especially on the French side. My favourite month is September as it is not as hot and dusty as July and August and there are not as many people about. In the second part of the month you risk being caught by an early snowstorm, as I once was (*see* page 31).

EQUIPMENT

Sleeping Bags and Tents

If you use staffed huts where meals are available (only possible on some of the walks), you can travel light, just carrying clothing and food and a few safety items. For the more basic unstaffed huts you will need a sleeping bag, an insulating mat (you may have to sleep on the floor), cooking gear and food as well.

However, on several of the walks, camping on at least some nights is essential. As the Pyrenees contain marvellous places for wild camping, and abound with magnificent potential sites, and because I have always camped, I have described the routes on the basis that tents rather than huts will be used. If you mostly use huts you might manage with just a 'breathable' fabric bivouac bag for the few nights you spend out, though these pose problems for cooking and eating when it rains, as it always seems to do when I use one. Those camping every night will need a lightweight backpacking tent of which there are many suitable models. As many sites are above the timberline and quite exposed to wind, tents with plenty of guylines and pegging points are a good idea. Temperatures can drop below freezing even in the middle of summer, though this is unusual, so a sleeping bag that will keep you warm in temperatures as low as –5°C (24°F) and an insulating mat are needed.

Stoves

It is possible to light camp fires in many places but great care should be taken to leave no trace when doing so. Live wood should never be cut. Too many meadows and glades are marred by rings of blackened stones and

A chough.

patches of charcoal and too many trees have been stripped of their lower limbs for it to be ethical for campers to rely on fires for warmth or hot food. Gone are the days when you could do all your cooking over a fire, as Showell Styles describes doing in his book *Backpacking in the Alps and Pyrenees*, without harming the environment. Today, fires should be regarded as luxuries and stoves always carried. Any light-weight stove will do, but if you intend to buy fuel during your trek, note that resealable butane cartridges, Coleman-type stove fuel and kerosene/paraffin are not easy to find but that most places sell the blue S200 Camping Gaz cartridges and fuel for methylated spirits/alcohol stoves (under the names *alcohol à bruler*, *alcohol denature* or *alcohol methylique* in France and *alcohol metilico* in Spain). Automobile fuel is readily available, of course, but not all so-called petrol stoves will run on this. My advice for trips of two weeks or less is to take all the fuel you will need with you.

Clothing

Clothing should be adequate for protection against rain, wind and cold, although for much of the time shorts and T-shirt can be worn, with a sun hat being a good idea for the hottest weather. The layer system is best, there being no need for heavy, filled jackets. Fabrics should be lightweight, durable, comfortable, quick drying, warm when wet, easy to wash, 'breathable' and, for outerwear, wind- and waterproof. In my opinion, pile and fleece garments, of which there are now myriad varieties and styles, are best for warm wear; thermal materials, such as wool, silk, Dunova, polypropylene, treated polyester, Chlorofibre or similar, for T-shirts and long underwear (not cotton, it is cold when wet), and polycotton or one of the new microfibres such as Tactel, Finesse, Climaguard, Technique, Supplex or Pertex for long trousers and windproof jackets. Waterproofs are more comfortable if made from a 'breathable' fabric such as Sympatex or Gore-tex. I now only carry a lightweight one in the Pyrenees as I have found it spends most of the time in the pack, the region being mostly dry in summer. In combination with a thin windproof top, this gives me as much protection in the occasional bout of prolonged wet weather as a heavier and bulkier jacket, and I can wear either layer on its own. Although the climate is mostly kind, minor items such as a warm hat and gloves or mitts are needed and can make all the difference between comfort and misery when it is wet and cold.

Your footwear is very important. For most of the treks, including those involving ascents of high peaks, lightweight boots or even shoes are best, there being no point in hauling heavy lumps of leather along dry trails and ending each day with hot, blistered feet (devotees of traditional boots will disagree vehemently with these sentiments, I know, but I find light-weight boots the most comfortable and I can only recommend what works for me). However, for the ascent of Pico de Aneto, crampons are needed so boots must be stiff enough for these and there could be enough snow or ice early in the season on peaks such as Monte Perdido and Pico de Posets for crampons to be needed then, as well. If you do take crampons, make sure they fit your boots properly and that you know how to use them before you go. Technical climbing crampons are not needed, the ones designated walkers' crampons are perfectly adequate.

Socks are also important. I carry at least three pairs of medium-weight ones, always keeping one pair dry and clean for wearing in camp. I prefer wool for socks but there are now a number of good synthetic alternatives available for those who find it itchy. I also find the traditional Ragg variety far superior to the

A Lammergeyer vulture.

more common loopstitch ones, as the soles of the latter matt down very quickly and need washing every day or so, which is hardly practical on a long backpacking trek.

Climbing Equipment

As most of the glaciers and snowfields you are likely to cross are gently angled, a standard walking or mountaineering ice axe is all you need, modern short climbing axes not being much use on this sort of terrain. I prefer a long staff or ski stick to an ice axe anyway, as it can be used for balance when crossing steep scree and boulder fields as well as snow and to take some of the weight on long ascents. They are especially useful with a heavy pack and I now take one on every trip. However, an ice axe should be carried for the Aneto glacier crossing and perhaps elsewhere earlier in the season when extensive snowfields may be encountered.

Other than ice axes and crampons, a rope should be carried if the Aneto glacier is to be crossed and it could be useful on the ascent of Pico de Posets. More difficult ascents requiring technical equipment are beyond the scope of this book.

The usual incidentals (first-aid kit, wash kit, torch, water bottle, bivvy bag, trail guides, maps, etc.) make up the rest of the load. Early in the season, insect repellent can be useful especially for treks in the lower, damp French valleys where mosquitoes and horse flies can be a problem.

Even with camping gear, you should not need to carry more than 18–20kg (40–44lb) on any of these treks and considerably less than that on most. Those using staffed huts should be able to keep the load below 7kg (15½lb) and not need a pack bigger than 40–45 litres in capacity. Back-packers will need a larger model, however, and, as those with any experience will know, the fit is very important. As many of the walks involve crossing steep, rough terrain and some involve a degree of scrambling, a body-hugging style of pack that does not upset the balance is a good idea. Internal-framed packs are best for this and I use one in the 70–100 litre range. Packs with removable pockets and compression straps (often called climbing sacks) can be reduced in size most easily for use as daypacks on side trips and ascents away from a camp which you might make.

HEALTH/MEDICAL

The big health threat is from the water. Although all water is suspect, I regularly drink that found above habitations (including mountain huts) and herds of livestock without treating it and, so far, have suffered no ill effects from so doing. The only time I have had diarrhoea from a Pyrenean trip was after the Haute Ariège walk when I rashly drank untreated water on the valley section even though there were farms above me. Boiling water is the surest way to kill any dangerous organisms but is hardly practical for all one's drinking needs. Chemical purification is a more convenient method. Of the two types, iodine tablets such as Potable Aqua are reckoned to be more effective than chlorine ones. Either sort make water taste foul, so fruit crystals or power are essential to mask this. The latest, and perhaps best, method of ensuring clean drinking water is to filter it and there are now a number of lightweight filters available.

To help minimize the spread of illness-creating organisms, great care should be taken with the deposition of faeces. In particular, toilets should be sited at least 200 metres (220yd) from any water, and faeces buried a few inches below the surface. For digging the necessary 'cathole', I carry a small plastic trowel. Toilet paper should be burned if this can be done safely, and the ashes buried. If possible, natural materials (snow is suprisingly efficient and pleasant!) should be used instead.

Sunburn is the other potential health hazard, and an ample supply of sunscreen should be carried. The southerly latitude and greater height of the Pyrenees means that the sun is far stronger than in the British hills. For those who really suffer from the heat, a sun hat and dark glasses (needed for glacier crossings anyway) may prove useful. Drinking copious amounts of water on hot days is essential so a large water bottle, at least a litre (1¾ pint), size is needed.

MAPS AND GUIDEBOOKS

I have listed the relevant maps and guidebooks at the end of each chapter (*see also* Further Reading). The French maps are excellent, with footpaths and huts marked on them. The Spanish maps are not as good and can add a certain excitement to one's walking. Both can be obtained from the official British agents of the French and Spanish national surveys:

Robertson McCarta Ltd.,
122 King's Cross,
London WC1X 9DS.
Tel: 071–278 8276

For planning treks and a general overview of the range, the IGN Carte Touristique 1:100,000 maps 69 (Pau Bayonne), 70 (Pau Bagnères-de-Luchon), 71 (St-Gaudens Andorre) and 72 (Beziers Perpignan) are useful, though some areas south of the frontier are not covered. A note on nomenclature seems in order as there are a number of abbreviations and terms that will be unfamiliar to those visiting the area for the first time.

Abbreviations

CAF	Club Alpine Français
CEC	Centre excursionniste de Catalogne
EA	Editorial Alpina
EDF	Electricité de France
FEM	Federacion Espanola de Montanismo
FFM	Federation Français de la Montagne
GR 10	Grande Randonnée 10
HRP	Haute Randonnée Pyrénéene
IGN	Institut Geographique National
PNP/PN	Parc National des Pyrénées
TCF	Touring Club de France

Some Useful Geographical Terms

abri basic shelter or cabin

ague, aigue, aygue water

arribet small stream

artiga, artigue pasture, meadow, clearing in forest

barranc, barranco ravine

bal, bat valley

borde barn

boum mountain lake

cabane shepherd's hut

caillaouas scree slope

calm high, bare plateau

campana needle of rock

canau, canaou steep gully

cap summit

caperan rock tower

clôt deep pool or mountain bowl

collade wide saddle or pass

corral cattle enclosure

cortal shepherd's hut

coume narrow valley

estang, etang, estany mountain lake

estibe meadow

fag, fach, faig beech tree

font, fount spring, fountain

forat, fourat deep hole, cave

forc, fourc, fourcat forked

gave mountain stream

gourg, gourc deep lake

hont, hount spring, fountain

hourquette steep pass

ibon mountain lake

jasse a level pasture

marcadau, marcat market

neste mountain river

orri stone hut

oule, oulette mountain basin

Parador Spanish state-owned hotel

pas, passet, passe narrow or difficult section

pena, pene cliff or mountain crest

pla, plan plain or level ground

port, porteille, portillon mountain pass

prat, pradère meadow

punta rock pinnacle

quebe shelter beneath a rock

raillère scree chute

redoun rounded

rio, riu river

seil, seilh glacier

serre, sierra mountain massif

soum rounded summit

trou deep hole

tuc, tuqua, tozal steep cliff

val, vall, vallée valley

PHOTOGRAPHY

All the walks pass through incredibly beautiful and photogenic scenery and most walkers will carry a camera. While a compact is light and simple to use, the possibilities for good photography are limited. If you want more than snapshots I would recommend an SLR with a couple of lenses. I usually carry two SLR bodies, a 24mm lens and 28–70 and 70–210 zoom lenses plus a few filters, of which the most important is a polarizer. These days I carry a lightweight tripod, too, although most of the photographs in the book were taken handheld or with an improvised support. I suggest using a slow-speed film, ISO 100 being the fastest I use – any faster and grain is noticeable, and detail, contrast and colour saturation are lost. The photographs in the book were taken over an eight-year period and a variety of films were used. Currently, my preferences are for Fujichrome 50 and 100 and Agfachrome RS 50 and 100. Dawn and dusk are the best times for photography, and the mountain camper is well placed to take advantage of the light then. While on the move, it is important to have your camera gear ready to hand. If it is in your pack you will not take many pictures. I carry mine in padded CCS camera cases, one slung across my body and the other fastened to the pack. Small items travel in a bumbag worn back to front.

Colour print film is fairly easy to come by in the Pyrenees but transparency (slide) film is only available in the larger places. I would suggest taking all the films you think you will need plus half as much again (the Pyrenees are very photogenic!) from home.

Further Reading

TRAIL GUIDES

Battagel, Arthur, *Pyrenees West/Pyrenees East/ Pyrenees Andorra Cerdagne* (Gaston West Col)
Three-volume guide to the mountains. The climbs are not of great technical difficulty. Not as useful for the long distance walker as the Reynolds, though (see below).

Castle, Alan, *Across the Pyrenees: the GR10* (Cicerone Guide)
Useful if you want to carry complete maps rather than the abbreviated ones in the topo guide.

Reynolds, Kev, *Walks and Climbs in the Pyrenees* (Cicerone Press)
Excellent single-volume guide to the whole range. The climbs are all at the easy end of the grading system and within the reach of most adventurous walkers. Contains details of the High Route from Lescun to Andorra.

Schwarz, Roz (translator/editor), *Walking the Pyrenees: GR 10* (Robertson McCarta)
The French topo guide in English. Contains sections of 1:50,000 topo maps with the route clearly marked.

Veron, Georges, *Pyrenees High Level Route* (Gaston West Col)

Stage by stage guide to the HRP from the Atlantic to the Mediterranean with alternatives, translated from the French.

NARRATIVES

Cleare, John (editor), *Trekking Great Walks of the World* (Unwin Hyman)
Contains a chapter on a high-level route from Lescun to Andorra by Kev Reynolds.

Reynolds, Kev, *Classic Walks in the Pyrenees* (Oxford Illustrated Press)
A well-illustrated selection.

Reynolds, Kev, *Mountains of the Pyrenees* (Cicerone Press)
A general and historical introduction to the Pyrenees. Much useful information.

Styles, Showell, *Backpacking in Alps and Pyrenees* (Gollancz)
Contains an entertaining account of a trek from Ax-les-Thermes to Bagnères de Luchon.

Unsworth, Walt (editor), *Classic Walks of the World* (Oxford Illustrated Press)
Contains a chapter on the High-Level Route by Kev Reynolds.

Index